LIVING & WORK

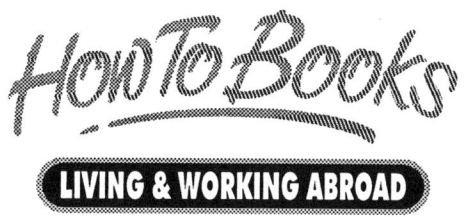

LIVING & WORKING IN ISRAEL

How to prepare for a successful
longterm stay

Ahron Bregman

KOSHER
BIKE CO.

How To Books

Cartoons by Mike Flanagan

British Library Cataloguing in Publication Data
A catalogue record for this book is available from the British Library.

© Copyright 1996 by Ahron Bregman.

First published in 1996 by How To Books Ltd, Plymbridge House,
Estover Road, Plymouth PL6 7PZ, United Kingdom.
Tel: (01752) 202301. Fax: (01752) 202331.

Note: The material contained in this book is set out in good faith for
general guidance and no liability can be accepted for loss or expense
incurred as a result of relying in particular circumstances on statements
made in the book. The laws and regulations are complex and liable to
change, and readers should check the current position with the relevant
authorities before making personal arrangements.

Produced for How To Books by Deer Park Productions.
Typeset by PDQ Typesetting, Stoke-on-Trent, Staffs.
Printed and bound by Cromwell Press, Broughton Gifford, Melksham,
Wiltshire.

Contents

List of Illustrations

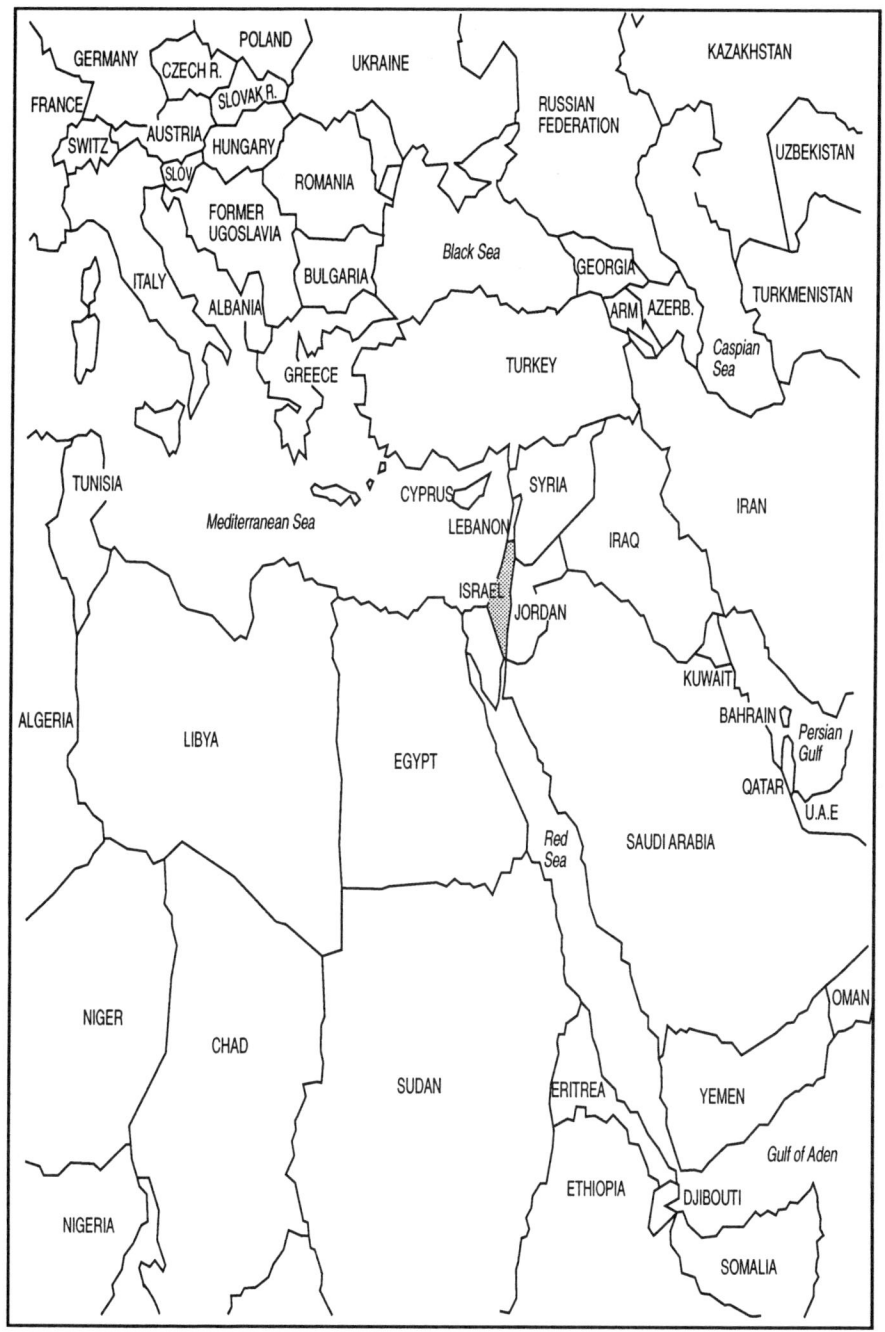

Fig. 1. Israel and its neighbours.

9

Preface

Israel has long been a popular destination for visitors. Many go there each year to travel, work on the Kibbutz or the Moshav, help with archaeological excavations, learn Hebrew or work in vacation jobs. With the advent of peace in the region, Israel is becoming even more attractive for those wishing to stay longer, work and do business with the Israelis. But you might find it hard adapting yourself to the place. The intensity and dynamism of Israeli life; the passionate and often impatient way Israelis express themselves; the hot summers and the language barrier – these might all cause you a bit of a shock (*Helem* in Hebrew).

Knowing in advance about potential difficulties and pitfalls and having some idea of how to cope with different situations might well soften your landing and improve your life there. This book will not only provide you with valuable information but also offer you a glimpse into life in Israel. When you have finished reading, tuck it into the bottom of your bag and use it as a reference source. You will always find some relevant information – a telephone number, an address, an idea or a piece of advice; and if that is not enough you could always use it to protect your head from the blazing sun!

Things are changing at in incredible speed in Israel and if you are going there I shall be glad to hear from you in order to update future editions. Keep in touch and send your comments to me, c/o How To Books, Plymbridge House, Estover Road, Plymouth PL6 7PZ, UK.

Be'hatzlacha – good luck!

Ahron Bregman

Is This You?

Student   Medical worker

Teacher

Agricultural worker   Au pair

Like to work with children

Young   Fit

Healthy

Free to travel   Available for work

Adaptable

Sociable   Tolerant

Outgoing personality

Reliable   Friendly

An inquiring mind

Ready for a challenge   Passport-holder

Businessman/business woman

Like the sun   Motivated

Want to live and work on a Kibbutz

Hotel manager   Archaeologist

Want to live and work in a Moshav

Self-disciplined   Bird-watcher

Looking for voluntary work

Fig. 2. Map of Israel.

12

1
Introducing Israel

GOING TO ISRAEL

In addition to being one of the most diverse and interesting tourist attractions of the world, Israel offers opportunities for the visitor who wishes to stay longer, work – voluntarily or non-voluntarily – do business and invest in the economy. But it is an illusion to think that in 'The Land of Milk and Honey', you might get a job, earn good money and settle down for a longer period without a good sweat. Whatever you choose to do in Israel, to succeed you need to understand the Israelis, work hard and above all be patient among the impatient. Knowledge of the language, or at least some basic words in Hebrew, though not a must could still help you especially in times of crisis.

LOOKING AT THE GEOGRAPHY AND CLIMATE

Israel stands at the crossroads of Asia, Africa and Europe. It is bounded to the west by the Mediterranean Sea, whose shoreline stretches along 117 miles; to the south by the Red Sea, whose coastline, mostly white sand, stretches along 6 miles; and to the east by the Great Syrian-African rift. Israel has a total area of 10,840 square miles within its boundaries and ceasefire lines.

The northern part of Israel, where most of the population and industry is concentrated, consists of three longitudinal strips. The most western is the coastline plain which runs parallel to the Mediterranean Sea and follows the shoreline in a southward widening band. The white-sandy shoreline is very narrow and is bordered by Kibbutzim, towns and the urban centres of Tel Aviv and Haifa.

Just east of the coastal plain are the western uplands: the hills of Galilee, the hills of Samaria and the hills of Judea which extend further south towards The Negev desert. The average height of these upland regions is 2,800ft and the main city in this sector is Jerusalem.

The most eastern longitudinal strip is the Jordan valley which is part of the great Syrian-African rift. The valley is bordered by the mountains of Judea and Samaria in the west and the mountains of Gila'ad and Moab in Jordan to the east.

The Jordan river (*Nehar Ha'Yarden*), of whose 176 miles 73 are in Israel, flows from sources in northern Galilee southward through the Jordan valley linking the two inland seas – the Sea of Galilee (*Yam Kinneret*) and the heavily saline Dead Sea (*Yam Ha'melach*) – which at -1,286 feet is the lowest spot on earth.

The southern part of the country is mainly desert (The Negev) but it is also very green especially around the settlements. The Negev comprises about half of the country's land area but it is inhabited by only 7 per cent of the population. The most important town is Be'er Sheva (Beersheba).

The capital of Israel is Jerusalem where most governmental offices (though not all foreign embassies) are concentrated; the commercial capital is Tel Aviv.

The climate
Israel enjoys long warm summers (April–October) and mild winters (November–March). The climate is generally temperate, although climatic conditions are varied across the country. The coldest month is January; the hottest August (see Fig. 3). The rainy season is from November until April with three-quarters of the annual rainfall between December and the end of February. Remember that:

• The hottest areas are those below sea level: the Jordan valley, the shores of the sea of Galilee, the shores of the Dead Sea and the valley of Beit Shean.

• The coldest areas (where in winter show falls occasionally) are the hills of Galilee, the Golan Heights and Jerusalem.

• The wettest area is Upper Galilee on the heights between Metulla and Sefad.

• The driest areas are the southern Negev and the Arava between the Dead Sea and the Gulf of Eilat.

• During the spring and autumn, periodic strong and dry easterly winds, called the *Hamssin*, increase the temperature (and the amount of dust you take into your lungs!).

	Jerusalem	Tel Aviv
Jan	42–53	48–64
Feb	43–57	47–65
Mar	47–60	51–68
Apr	53–69	54–72
May	59–77	63–77
June	63–81	66–82
July	65–83	69–86
Aug	65–83	71–86
Sep	64–81	68–88
Oct	60–77	59–83
Nov	54–66	54–76
Dec	46–56	47–66

Fig. 3. Average monthly temperatures (°F min-max)

- In summer it might be sweltering hot and humid in Tel Aviv but dry and cooler in Jerusalem.

- In Eilat and the desert areas there is year-round sunshine.

TIPS – WHAT TO PACK?

Generally the dress code is very casual all year around wherever you go.

March–May
You will need light cotton trousers and a short sleeved cotton shirt or T shirt, summer dresses and shorts for warmer days, a light jumper or cardigan for evenings and a light jacket if you are going out. Don't forget your swim wear and sun block!

June–August
Shorts and sleeveless shirts or T shirts and summer dresses. A light long sleeved shirt to wear over a dress at night would be useful. Sandles are a must and sun hats recommended.

September–October
Cotton trousers and short sleeved shirts or T shirts and light dresses

and a pair of shorts, as well as a light jumper or cardigan for evenings. Wear sandles or light leather shoes, but please don't wear stocks with your sandles. Swim wear, sunglasses and sun block still essential.

November–February

Trousers, leggings and layers of different jumpers, thick woolly socks and boots or trainers may be all you need in Tel Aviv. But a coat is recommended for Jerusalem, desert areas and the north. A raincoat and umbrella and a change of shoes are useful for soaked feet. Gloves and hat depending on your sensitivity to cold.

LOOKING AT THE ECONOMY

In 1996 Israel's per capita GDP (Gross Domestic Product) exceeded £9,066, placing it 21st among 200 countries in the world. Israel's growth was 7 per cent and unemployment relatively low.

Israel's international position in some areas of industrial and agricultural production capacity and exports is remarkable and it has free trade agreements with Europe and the USA. The Israeli economy is composed of three sectors: the public, the Histadrut and the private sector.

The public sector

This includes all economic units owned by the state. The government controls approximately two hundred enterprises, each legally defined as a corporation but in which voting shares are owned by government bodies or by the state. Some of these enterprises are very small and carry out peripheral activities; others are giants by Israeli standards. Examples are: Bank for Industrial Development; the oil refineries; the Be'zek Telephone and Telecommunications Company; Israel Chemicals; the Electricity Company; the Israeli Military Industries.

Through these enterprises the government holds a monopoly position in important fields including electricity and international air transportation. More than two-thirds of the Israeli work force is employed in the public sector. Since the mid-1970s, the government has been declaring its intention to privatise many of the enterprises it controls, although little has been done so far.

The Histadrut sector

This sector includes all the institutions and enterprises owned by Histadrut ('The Federation') which is the largest trade union organisation in Israel. The Histadrut is also involved in such areas as health, education and even foreign affairs. The Histadrut controls some of the biggest enterprises in Israel; examples are: **Solel Bo'neh** which is the largest construction firm in Israel, **Koor** which is composed of more than a hundred manufacturing plants and **Bank Ha'poalim** ('The Workers Bank') which is the largest bank in Israel.

The private sector
This sector is largely composed of small firms, many of which are family owned. A very large percentage of the private sector operates in a protective environment, created by a variety of administrative means, and in which an incumbent has entrenched rights. Many of these firms do not receive any government aid.

BRANCHES OF THE ECONOMY

Since independence there have been significant changes in the emphasis of the country's economy, including primarily the shift of investment from consumer industries to the more sophisticated production of electronic equipment and computers. Israel is now a world leader in the production of medical electronics, agro-technology, computer hardware and software, fine chemicals, diamond cutting and, unfortunately, weapons.

Agriculture
Since 1948 the total area under cultivation has increased by a factor of 2.6 to approximately 1.1 million acres and irrigated land has increased by a factor of 8 to about 0.6 million acres. However, the share of agricultural production in the GNP declined from 11 to 3.5 per cent between 1950 and 1994. The percentage of employees in agriculture is about 4.7 per cent of the Israeli work force.

Agriculture is centrally planned and regulated. Israel's farm production consists largely of dairy and poultry products as well as a large variety of flowers, fruit and vegetables. Today Israel meets most of its food needs through domestic production, supplemented by imports, mainly of grain, oilseeds, meat, coffee, cocoa and sugar.

Israeli agriculture has achieved world records in production of milk per cow and has been able to develop new varieties of fruit and vegetables, extend the shelf-life of many products, increase agricultural productivity and save water by inventing drip irrigation.

Manufacturing
The government considers this branch an important one and tries to accelerate the rate of growth of manufacturing. For political reasons, however, it prefers to encourage manufacturing not by low taxation but mainly in intervention, regulation and control of each and every firm. As a result close contacts with those having the authority to grant these concessions have been a most salient factor of production.

Construction
Once considered a leading economic activity and a barometer of the Israeli economy, the construction sector in the early 1990s contributed only 7 per cent to the GNP, down from 30 per cent in the early 1950s.

Up to 1975 the government was the major builder in Israel, building almost half of the flats. Since then, however, its share declined dramatically to about 18.3 per cent in the early 1990s. However, control of the land and the ability to allocate credit still make the government very influential in the construction market.

Energy
Despite hundreds of millions of dollars spent on oil, gas and coal exploration, very little has so far been discovered. During 1967–79 Israel produced oil in Sinai but after it pulled out of the desert it did not have its own sources of fuel.

In 1949 the large oil multinationals ceased their operations in Israel forcing the government to agree to the conditions imposed for the supply of energy. A fuel administration was established to represent the Israeli interests *vis-à-vis* the oil multinationals and in 1951 Israel established **The Delek** company which received the government's right for refining 30 per cent of Israel's consumption. Despite the importance of energy, only 10 per cent of the shares were held by the state until the mid-1970s and since then the share of the government has been reduced to 1 per cent; the rest of the ownership is equally divided between the private and the Histadrut sector at 45 per cent each.

Transportation and communications
The transport and communications sector in Israel employs 6 per cent of the country's labour force. About a fifth of the transportation, storage and communication output in Israel is in truck services, 19 per cent in buses and taxis, 3 per cent in railway services, 15 per cent

in sea transport, 19 per cent in post services, 9 per cent air transport and airport services, and 14 per cent in communications. Except for trucks owned by private firms, all of these are either owned by the government (air transportation, ports) or regulated by it (truck services, taxis, buses). Bus transportation is supplied in the main by monopoly Histadrut-controlled co-operatives.

Banking and the capital market

In the last forty years or so, the Israeli banking system has gone through a continuous process of concentration and a sharp decrease in the number of banking institutions. The credit co-operatives were the first to go and small banks disappeared or were swallowed by the big three groups: Bank Leumi, Bank Ha'poalim and the Discount Bank which, since the mid-1970s, accounted for more than 90 per cent of all deposits or banking assets. This process was encouraged by the Bank of Israel, which is the central bank controlling all the banks and whose governor is also the economic adviser to the government.

Israeli banks are extremely diversified, supplying a wide range of services in Israel and abroad. Since 1985, the government and the Bank of Israel have allowed the banks more discretion and have deregulated commissions.

All credit flows in the capital market are regulated by the government. The financial institutions are intermediaries between the savers who supply the capital and the government and business firms that need the capital. The government also controls most of the funds received from foreign sources. The government may also ban the use of any foreign credit or make it more expensive by levying taxes.

Addresses of commercial organisations
Bank of Israel, Governor: Prof. Y. Frenkel, Eliezer Kaplan Street, Kiryat Ben Gurion, Jerusalem. Tel: 02 6552211.
Israel-British Chamber of Commerce, Secretary General: F. Kipper, 76 Iben Gvirol Street, Tel Aviv, 64162. Tel: 03 6959732.
Histadrut – General Federation of Labour in Israel, Secretary General: H. Ramon, 93 Arloseroff Street, Tel Aviv, 62098. Tel: 03 6921111, 6921630. Telex: 342488 HISTD IL. Fax: (972) 3 69 69 906.
Manufacturers' Association of Israel, President: D. Lautman, Jerusalem PO Box 526. Tel: 02 6231057. Haifa PO Box 639. Tel: 04 8524202. Tel Aviv PO Box 29116. Tel: 03 5198787.

Israel and British Commonwealth Association, Secretary: D. Jacobson, 76 Iben Gvirol Street, Tel Aviv, PO Box 4090. Tel: 03 6265244.
Federation of Israeli Chambers of Commerce, PO Box 20027, 84 Ha'hashmonaim Street, Tel Aviv, 67011. Tel: 03 5612444. Fax: 03 5612614. Telex: 33484 (a/b CHCOM IL).

UNDERSTANDING THE POLITICAL SITUATION

The State of Israel is a parliamentary democracy. It has no written constitution but a number of 'Basic Laws' which, in due course, are supposed to be incorporated into a written constitution.

The official head of state is the **President** (*Nasi* in Hebrew) who is elected by the parliament (the *Knesset* in Hebrew) for a five-year term by a simple majority. The present President is Ezer Weizmann whose uncle Haim Weizmann was the first President of the State of Israel.

The main duties of the President are to receive foreign diplomats, sign treaties, appoint judges, appoint the governor of the Bank of Israel and heads of Israel's diplomatic missions abroad (on recommendation of the appropriate bodies) and pardon prisoners and commute sentences (on advice of the Minister of Justice).

Parliament

The Knesset, which is the Israeli parliament, took its name and fixed its membership at 120 from the *Knesset Ha'gedolah*, the representative Jewish body convened in Jerusalem by Ezrea and Nehemiah in the fifth century BCE.

Members of the Knesset are elected for a period of four years by all citizens aged 18 and over, using a system of proportional representation. The Knesset's function is to legislate and to oversee the workings of the government. It operates in plenary sessions and through ten standing committees.

Knesset debates are conducted in Hebrew, but members may speak Arabic, as both are official languages. In plenary sessions, general debates are conducted on government policy and activity, as well as on legislation submitted by the government or individual Knesset members. To become law, a bill must pass three readings in the Knesset. After the first reading, it is referred to the appropriate committee for discussion; at the second, it is reviewed in plenary session; at the third, a final vote is taken. The minister concerned, the Prime Minister and the President sign the bill into law.

Executive
The government, headed by the Prime Minister (at present Benyamin Netanyahu) and another eighteen ministers, most of whom head governmental ministries, functions as the executive body. It is collectively responsible to the Knesset whose confidence it must enjoy. The government usually serves for four years, but its term of office may be shortened by the resignation or death of the Prime Minister, or a vote of no confidence by the Knesset.

Judiciary
The Israeli **courts** are independent and in matters of personal status each religious group has its own jurisdiction. Judges are appointed by the President upon recommendation of a special nine-person committee composed of three Supreme Court justices, two members of the Israeli Bar and four public figures. Judges receive appointments for life, with retirement at the age of 70.

Audit
A **State Comptroller** appointed by the President is responsible only to the Knesset. He provides a continuous independent audit of governmental finances and transactions, makes recommendations for administrative efficiency and investigates charges of corruption against government officials.

The political parties
Israel has a multiple-party system reflecting a wide range of outlooks and beliefs. No political party has ever received an absolute majority and all governments, so far, have been coalitions. Usually the small religious parties hold the balance of political power in the formation of government coalitions.

The two main parties are **Labour** which is left of centre and holds social democratic views and the **Likud** bloc which is right of centre, holding centrist and nationalist views. The leader of Labour is Shimon Peres; the leader of Likud is Benyamin Netanyahu who is also the Prime Minister.

The Labour bloc was in power from the establishment of the state in 1948 until 1977, the year the Likud led by Menachem Begin won the elections and formed a government. The Likud remained until 1992 when it was defeated by the Labour party in the general elections. In 1996 the Likud was elected again.

Other parties represented in the Knesset are: National Religious Party, Agudat Yisrael, Se'pharadi Torah Guardians (Shas), Ha'dash,

Shinui (Change), Tzomet (Junction) party, Arab Democrats, Mo'ledet, The Third Way, Yisrael Be'alia.

Addresses of parties
Israel Labour Party, 110 Ha'yarkon Street, Tel Aviv. Tel: 03 5209222.
The Likud, Metsudat Ze'ev, 38 King George Street, Tel Aviv. Tel: 03 6210666.
National Religious Party, 4 Markin Street, Ramat Gan. Tel: 03 6702541.
Agudat Yisrael, 5 Harav Orenstein Yitzhak, Jerusalem. Tel: 02 5384357.
Se'pharadi Torah Guardians (Shas), 20 Aliav Street, Jerusalem. Tel: 02 5371786.
Ha'dash, 17 Tirtza Street, Tel Aviv. Tel: 03 6835252.
Shinui, 22 Mikve Yisrael, Tel Aviv. Tel: 03 3614737.
Tzomet, 44 Derech Petach Tikva, Tel Aviv. Tel: 03 6393786.
Mo'ledet, 23 Ha'melech George, Jerusalem. Tel: 02 6249195.
The Third Way, 8 Kaplan Street, Tel Aviv. Tel: 03 6950052.
Yisrael Be'aliya, 40 Derech Petach, Tikva, Tel Aviv. Tel: 03 6874998.

War and peace
Since its establishment in 1948 Israel has been in a permanent situation of war with its Arab neighbours. The Israeli Defence Forces (IDF) were involved in six major wars: 1948–49, 1956, 1967, 1968–70, 1973, 1982 and in quelling disturbances in the occupied territories (the **Intifada**) between 1987 and 1993. In 1979 Israel signed a peace treaty with Egypt and in return for peace agreed to withdraw its forces from the Sinai Peninsula which it had occupied in 1967.

A complicated problem has always been that of the **Palestinians**, many of whom left Palestine during the first Arab-Israeli war of 1948. For many years the PLO, which is the political body representing the Palestinians, has refused to recognise the state of Israel (calling it 'The Zionist Entity') and resorted to terrorism against Israelis. Israel, in turn, refused to recognise the PLO as the representative of the Palestinians and used military means to defeat Palestinian terrorism in Israel and abroad.

Following the elections of 1992, Yitzhak Rabin's government recognised the PLO as the legitimate body representing the Palestinians and the PLO recognised the state of Israel and agreed to cease using terrorism as a means to achieve its political aims.

An agreement was signed between Israel and the PLO in 1993 leading to Israeli withdrawal from Gaza and Jericho. Later Israeli forces pulled out from other West Bank cities and towns. In 1993 peace was also signed between Israel and Jordan. Negotiations are under way to achieve peace between Israel and Syria and Lebanon.

Israeli Defence Force (IDF)

The IDF was founded in 1948. The three service branches of the IDF (Ground Forces, Air Force, Navy) function under a unified command headed by the Chief of Staff who at present is Amnon Shahak.

All eligible men and women are drafted at age 18. Men serve for three years, women for two. Upon completion of compulsory service, each solider is assigned to a reserve unit. Men up to age 51 serve about 30 days a year, which in times of emergency can be increased to 60 days or even more. Single women are liable for reserve duty, usually up to age 24 or until having children. Any man or woman having completed compulsory service and meeting current IDF needs may sign up for the standing army. Career soldiers are eligible for retirement after 20 years of service.

KNOWING THE PEOPLE

The total population of Israel in 1996 is 5,570,000, composed of 9 main groups: Jews, Arabs, Christians, Druze, Black Hebrews, Karaites, Baha'is, Samaritans and Circassians. Figure 4 shows the population figures of some urban centres.

Jews

This is the largest ethnic group consisting of 4,510,000 people (81 per cent of the total population). The traditional division of the Jews is between **As'hkenazim**, who came or are descendants of Jews from Central and Eastern Europe (**Yiddish**, based on an older form of German, used to be their language) and **Se'pharadim** who are descendents of the Jews expelled from Spain and Portugal in the fifteenth century. Nowadays the term Se'pharadim is applied to all Oriental Jews.

Other Jewish immigrants came to Israel from Africa (mainly from Morocco), Asia (mainly from Iraq, Iran, Yemen and Turkey) and from America. The last two waves of immigrants to Israel came from Ethiopia but mainly from the former USSR. In 1996 more than 78,000 Jews, 86 per cent of the total immigration to Israel that year, arrived from the former USSR.

The majority of Jews/Israelis living in Israel at present were born

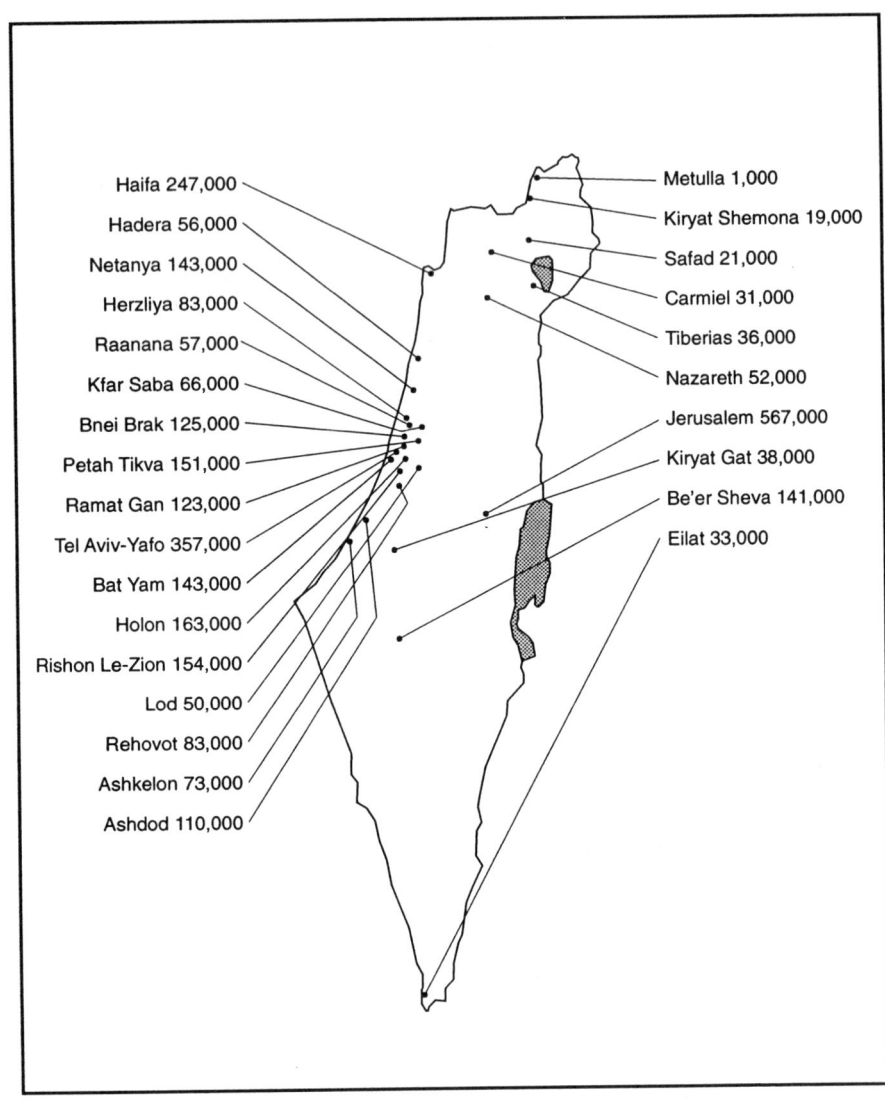

Haifa 247,000
Hadera 56,000
Netanya 143,000
Herzliya 83,000
Raanana 57,000
Kfar Saba 66,000
Bnei Brak 125,000
Petah Tikva 151,000
Ramat Gan 123,000
Tel Aviv-Yafo 357,000
Bat Yam 143,000
Holon 163,000
Rishon Le-Zion 154,000
Lod 50,000
Rehovot 83,000
Ashkelon 73,000
Ashdod 110,000

Metulla 1,000
Kiryat Shemona 19,000
Safad 21,000
Carmiel 31,000
Tiberias 36,000
Nazareth 52,000
Jerusalem 567,000
Kiryat Gat 38,000
Be'er Sheva 141,000
Eilat 33,000

Fig. 4. Population figures for some urban centres.

in the country. They are known as **Sabras**, which is the name of a prickly, but very sweet, fruit, thus symbolising the Israelis who are known to be prickly on the outside but sweet on the inside.

Arabs

Israel's non-Jewish population is overwhelmingly Arab and most of the Arabs are Moslems; the remainder are Christians. The total number of Moslems living in Israel in 1996 is 805,000 (14.4 per cent of the total population) and the majority of them were born in the country and remained during and after the first Arab-Israeli war while others left. They reside mainly in small towns and villages, over half of them in Galilee.

Nearly 10 per cent of Israel's Arabs are Bedouins, tribes of traditional nomadic people who still live in tents and keep sheep, goats and camels. They belong to about 30 tribes, most of them scattered over a wide area in the Negev. Encouraged by the Israeli government many of the Bedouins now live in permanent villages.

Christians
The number of Christians living in Israel in 1996 is 160,000 (2.9 per cent of the total population). Among the Christians there are Arabs, Armenians, foreign clergymen, monks and those working for Christian organisations. Most of the Christians live in Jerusalem but there are also some groups in Haifa and Galilee.

Druze
There are 95,000 Druze in Israel (1.7 per cent of the total population), most of whom live in a few villages in Galilee and on Mount Carmel. There are also Druze villages on the Golan Heights which are likely to be returned to Syrian hands when a peace treaty is signed between Israel and Syria.

While the Druze religion is not accessible to outsiders, one known aspect of its philosophy is the concept of *Taqiyya*, which calls for complete loyalty by its adherents to the government of the country in which they reside. The Druze are considered very loyal to Israel and, unlike the Israeli-Arabs, they serve in the army.

Black Hebrews
The first Hebrews arrived in Israel in 1969 and claimed to be the most authentic descendants of the Jews exiled from Israel 4,000 years ago. They number around 1,200 and most of them live in the southern town of Dimona.

Karaites
This Jewish sect of about 15,000 members dates back to the ninth century. Its members profess strict adherence to **The Torah**, which is the five books of Moses, and reject rabbinic tradition. The Karaites lived in the Jewish quarter of Jerusalem until 1948 and when the quarter fell into Jordanian hands they were forced to leave. The Karaites now live in Ashdod, Be'er Sheva and Ramla.

Baha'is

The world of centre of Baha'i faith is in the northern town of Haifa. Some of these people are descended from the Baha'i group which was expelled from Persia in 1863 to the Ottoman Empire.

Samaritans

This is believed to be the smallest ethnic group in the world. The Samaritans are first mentioned in the Bible at the beginning of the Second Temple era. They regard themselves as the true Jews faithful only to The Torah and its immediate sequel, the Book of Joshua. Mount Gerizim in Samaria is their holy site which they believe was the location of the Temple.

The Samaritans claim descent from the tribes of Joseph and his sons Menasseh and Ephraim. There are two Samaritan communities numbering together approximately 550 people; one group lives in Nablus on the West Bank, the other in the town of Holon which is just south-east of Tel Aviv.

The Samaritans speak Arabic and use an archaic form of Hebrew in their liturgy.

Circassians

This Muslim community numbering some 4,000 arrived in Palestine in the 1890s from the Caucasian Mountains in Russia and live today in Galilee. They are Sunni Muslims, although they share neither the Arab origin nor the cultural background of the larger Islamic community. While Arabic is still used for everyday communication, it is gradually being replaced by Hebrew among the youth, along with Circassian language.

DISCUSSION POINTS

1. How will you balance your personal flexibility regarding travel time with climate considerations to decide **when** to go to Israel and to **where**?

2. Now that you know when to go to Israel and to where, try to decide what you want to pack. The tips on page 15 can be useful.

3. You wish to join the Israeli labour market. First decide to which *sector* of the Israeli economy you (or rather your profession or interest) fits. Then be more specific and identify which *branch* of the economy you fit the best.

2
Getting There and Travelling Around

SORTING OUT THE PAPERWORK AND MONEY MATTERS

Visas and work permit

No visa is required if you hold a full British passport or if you are a citizen of Northern Ireland, the Channel Islands or the Isle of Man. Your passport must have at least six months to run after the date you enter Israel. For specific enquiries contact the Consulate section of the Embassy of Israel. *Address*: 2 Palace Green, London W8 4QB. Tel: (0171) 957 9517.

On arrival you will probably get a tourist visa for a period of three months. If you enter through the land borders, either from Egypt or from Jordan, you might get only one month's stay. It is useful to keep a photocopy of the pages of your passport which carry your personal details and the visa stamp just in case you lose your passport and need to prove that you had a valid passport and a visa.

Getting an extension

If after your initial three months' stay in Israel you wish to stay longer, you need to apply for an extension of your visa. If you wish to work you will need a B/1 visa. You can apply in one of the Ministry of Interior offices which are usually open at 0800. Expect a long queue especially in the big cities. You will be required to fill in an application form, have a passport-size photo and prove that you have enough money to stay longer. A return ticket and a reference letter could always help you to get the extension.

If all is well you will get, for a nominal fee, a three-month extension to the initial three months.

• Avoid mentioning the words 'work' or 'job' when applying for an extension.

If you work on a Kibbutz or Moshav they will arrange for visas and

27

if you are a valued worker you should be able to get lengthy extensions. If you work as an au pair or in any other job, let the family with whom you work or the agency which placed you arrange an extension of your visa.

The **addresses** of offices of the Ministry of Interior where you can apply for an extension of your visa are:

Jerusalem – 1 Shlomzion Ha'malka Street. Tel: 02 6290222.
Tel Aviv – Shalom Tower, 9 Ahad Ha'am Street. Tel: 03 5193333.
Haifa – 11 Hassan Shuqri Street. Tel: 04 8616222.

You can also extend your visa in the district commission offices of the following towns: Afulla, Akko (Acre), Ashkelon, Be'er Sheva, Eilat, Hadera, Herzliyya, Holon, Nazareth Illit, Netanya, Petah Tiqva, Ramat Gan, Rehovot, Sefad, Tiberias.

Money matters

The Israeli currency is the shekel (IS), also called the New Israeli Shekel (NIS); plural: shekalim. Each shekel is divided into 100 agorot (singular: agora). Bank notes circulate in denominations of 200, 100, 50, 20 and 10 sheqalim and coins in denominations of 5 shekalim, 1 shekel and 50 and 10 agorot.

The shekel was known as early as the second millennium BCE as a unit of weight for means of payment in gold and silver. It is recorded in the Bible that Abraham negotiated the purchase of a field and a cave at Machpela near Hebron saying: 'I will give thee money for the field; take it of me, and I will bury my dead there.' Ephron, the landowner, replied: 'The land is worth four hundred shekels of silver...and Abraham weighed to Ephron...four hundred shekels of silver, current money with the merchant' (Genesis 23:13, 15–17).

You can bring an unlimited amount of local and foreign currency into Israel in cash, travellers' cheques, letters of credit. Sterling and especially dollars are widely accepted throughout the country, as well as all leading credit cards. You can draw cash from most banks with Visa, Master Card, Access, Eurocard and American Express card. Remember that payment of extra bills and tours in foreign currency exempts you from VAT. You can also open your own local currency account or special non-resident foreign currency account at any bank.

Most banks are open: Sunday, Monday, Tuesday and Thursday from 0830 to 1230 and from 1600 to 1730. Wednesday from 0830 to

1230. Friday and eve of holy days from 0830 to 1200 pm.

ARRIVING IN ISRAEL

You can get to Israel by air, land or sea.

Arriving by air
There are daily flights to Israel from both Heathrow and Gatwick airports, as well as from other airports across the country such as Luton and Manchester. El Al (LY), the Israeli national airline, and British Airways (BA) fly from both Heathrow and Gatwick and a flight to Israel's national airport, Ben Gurion, takes 4 hours 30 minutes. If you fly to Eilat it will take you 5 hours. (Remember that for most of the year there is a two-hour time difference with the UK.)

Air fares vary considerably according to season with the most expensive flight tickets during the months July to September and Jewish holidays. Charter flights are much cheaper but you have to remember that most charter flights leave from Gatwick, Luton and Manchester which means that if, for example, you leave from central London you will need to buy a relatively expensive rail ticket to get to the airport.

It is worth shopping around to find the best deal. Check the ads, especially in the weekly *Jewish Chronicle* which you can find in the big book stores (WH Smith, Dillons and others) and also in the Sunday papers. STA, the students' travel agency, usually offers good deals. It is also worth trying West End Travel (see below).

If you want to fly your own plane you should provide the Israeli Airports Authority with all mandatory information at least 48 hours in advance via cable, AFTN message, telex or fax and await clearance before commencing the flight.

Useful telephones and addresses
The Air Travel Advisory Bureau (for free advice on air travel). Tel: (0171) 636 5000 (London) or (0161) 832 2000 (Manchester).
West End Travel Ltd, Barratt House, 341 Oxford Street, London W1R 1HB. Tel: (0171) 629 6299 (main switchboard); (0171) 409 0630 (Israel Department).
El Al. Tel: (0171) 437 8237.
British Airways. Tel: (0181) 759 5511.
STA, the students' travel agency.Tel: 02 6222333 (Jerusalem); (0171) 361 6161 (London).
Ben Gurion International Airport. Tel: 03 9710000; recorded arrival

and departure: 03 972 3333; 03 9710111.
Ovda Airport (south). Tel: 07 6375880.
Eilat Airport (south). Tel: 07 6371828.
Israel Airports Authority, PO Box 137, Ben Gurion International
  Airport, 70100, Lod. Tel: 03 9710000. Fax: 03 9721217. Telex:
  381003 TELCO IL. Cable address: MEMTEUFA BENGURION
  AIRPORT.

Arriving by land
You can enter Israel by land from either Egypt or Jordan. There are
two crossing points from **Egypt** into Israel: Rafiah (Rafah) and
Taba which are open all year round, seven days a week except for
Yom Kippur and the first day of the Moslem Feast of Id El Adha.
  Rafiah, the main point of entry, is located some 30 miles south-
west of Ashkelon and is open from 0900 to 1700. If you are crossing
the border by car you must present a valid driving licence and
carnet-de-passage.

• Remember that you cannot cross the border using a rented car.

  Egged, the Israeli bus company, runs its no. 362 bus which leaves
Tel Aviv for the Rafiah terminal daily at 0850 and Rafiah for Tel
Aviv at 1500. Another Egged bus which runs between Tel Aviv and
Cairo is no. 100 which leaves Tel Aviv for Cairo and Cairo for Tel
Aviv daily at 0800.
  The crosscheck at **Taba** which is very close to Eilat is open 24
hours a day and can be crossed on foot. If you wish to cross through
Taba you will have to make your way either by bus or by other
means of transportation across the Sinai Peninsula. If you intend to
visit southern Sinai you can obtain a special Egyptian visa at the
border, valid for two weeks only. A departure fee is charged. For
visas of longer duration you need to apply at the Egyptian consulate
at Eilat or Tel Aviv. Egged bus no. 15 provides a regular service
from Eilat to the Taba terminal and back.

*Useful addresses of bus companies in Cairo which operate buses to
Israel*
Eastern Delta Transportation Co, Abassiya Station. Tel: 839589,
  824773.
Isis Travel, 48 Giza Street. Tel: 3484821, 3487761.
Traco, 13 Sharia Mahmoud Azmy. Tel: 3420488.

Coming to Israel from **Jordan** you can cross at the **Allenby Bridge**, near Jericho, which is only 25 miles from Jerusalem. It is open for tourists on the Israeli side from Sunday to Thursday from 0800 to 2300, on Fridays and Saturdays from 0800 to 1400 and the eve of major holidays from 0800 to 1000. On Yom Kippur the bridge is closed. A border tax is levied for entering and leaving Israel and may be paid at the bridge. You can catch an Egged bus or a taxi which will take you from the crossing point to Jerusalem from where you can travel to other parts of the country.

• Remember that no private vehicles are permitted to cross.

You can also cross through the **Arava** checkpoint which is about 3 miles north of Eilat. Egged bus no. 16 leaves every hour from the central bus station in Eilat to the Arava checkpoint and returns. The opening hours for the Arava border checkpoint are 0630 to 2200 Monday to Thursday; Friday, Saturday, 0800 to 2000; Yom Kippur and the Jordanian festival on the first day of the Hijirah Calender, closed. Transfer of passengers between the Israeli and Jordanian checkpoints is carried out by shuttle service and transfer on foot is not permitted.

Useful telephone numbers

Border crossing Egypt	The Rafiah Terminal. Tel: 07 6734205. The Taba Terminal. Tel: 07 6373110; 07 6372104.
Border crossing Jordan	Allenby Bridge. Tel: 02 9942302. Arava. Tel: 07 6336811.
The Egyptian Consulate	Tel: 07 6376882 (Eilat).
The Egyptian Embassy	54 Bazel Street, Tel Aviv. Tel: 03 5464151/2.

Arriving by sea

You can also reach Israel via the ferry service from Piraeus, near Athens, to Isreal's northern port in Haifa; the trip takes about 58 hours. There are also cruise lines which leave Italy (Brindisi, Bari, Ancona and more) and other Mediterranean ports to sail to Haifa. Cunard operate cruises in the eastern Mediterranean starting from Venice, then sailing to Alexandria, stopping at Ashdod and Haifa, then up to Athens. If you come from Egypt you can take one of the ferries of Grimaldi/Siosa Lines which run between Alexandria and the Israeli port of Ashdod. If you are a student you can get a cheap ticket.

If you wish to enter Israel with your own craft you can do so via the ports of Haifa, Ashdod or Eilat or the Tel Aviv Marina. You will have to pass border and customs clearance and then proceed to any of Israel's four special yacht marinas. Remember to contact the marina of your choice and reserve a place several weeks in advance, providing full particulars concerning your vessel.

Useful telephone numbers: yacht marinas
Atarim (Tel Aviv). Tel: 03 5254276.
Yaffo (Jaffa). Tel: 03 6820772.
Akko (Acre) Tel: 04 9919287. Fax: 04 913889.
Eilat. Tel: 07 6367186.

LANDING AND GETTING TO YOUR FINAL DESTINATION

Most visitors arrive by air at the country's main international air terminal, Ben Gurion, which is 12 miles east of Tel Aviv and 31 miles west of Jerusalem. On arrival the majority head for either Tel Aviv or Jerusalem.

When your plane touches down you will hear a faint applause. This is an Israeli tradition (adopted from the French) to applaud the safe landing. The next thing you see is people, some Israelis but mainly religious people (who are always in a hurry), taking their belongings (ignoring the fact that the aircraft is still on the move!) and heading towards the closed doors. You can remain seated; the bus which is to take you the two-minute drive from the plane's door to the terminal will wait for you.

At the checkpoint you will have to present your passport and entry forms to be stamped by the passport control official (usually a pleasant young woman who has just completed her military service). If you plan to go to an Arab state with whom Israel has no diplomatic relations ask the official, *before submitting your document,* not to have your passport stamped. You will get the stamp and visa on a separate sheet.

With your passport stamped (**remember**: you are a tourist so do not mention the words: 'job' or 'work') you cross the checkpoint. On your right-hand side you see the money exchange.

• Remember: banks are closed on holidays, at weekends, as well as on the afternoons of Wednesday and Friday. If you think you will need any money, change now.

Further to your right you can see the tourist information desk. If you need accommodation they can help you find it.

Passing through customs

The dual-channel customs clearance system is in operation at Israel's airports. If you have no goods to declare you can pass through the Green channel on leaving the arrivals hall. If you are bringing in other items, even if exempt from duty, you must declare them and use the Red channel.

If you are aged 17 years and over you are allowed to import into Israel, without paying customs duties, the following items: 250 cigarettes or 250 g of tobacco products; 2 litres of wine, 1 litre of spirits, 250 ml of eau de cologne or perfume; gifts up to the value of £100.

Useful address
The Department of Customs, 32 Agron Street, 91002, Jerusalem. Tel: 02 6703333.

Pets

If you take your dog or cat with you, remember that they must be over four months old, have been inoculated against rabies and bear a valid official veterinary health certificate from the country of origin.

Getting to your final destination

Buses
If you crossed to Israel by land through either Egypt or Jordan, or came on ferry to either Ashdod or Haifa and you wish to travel to any specific place in the country, then the easiest way to do so is by **bus**. Get to the central bus station (*Tachana Merkazit* in Hebrew) in the nearest town/city and from there take another bus to your final destination. You could always ask for details in the station's information desk (*Modiyyin* in Hebrew).

Eilat
If you landed in Eilat you most probably intend to stay there for a while. The airport is centrally located within walking distance of the town's centre and you could easily walk to your destination or take a taxi.

	Jerusalem		Tel Aviv		Haifa		Tiberias		Be'er Sheva	
	km.	miles	km.	miles	km.	miles	km.	miles	km.	miles
Afula	146	91	91	57	41	25	41	25	206	128
Akko (Acre)	181	112	117	73	22	14	56	35	232	144
Arad	104	65	158	98	255	158	232	144	45	28
Ashqelon	73	45	63	39	160	99	197	122	67	42
Be'er Sheva	84	52	113	70	210	130	236	147	–	–
Bet She'an	120	70	117	73	67	42	37	23	198	123
Eilat	312	194	354	220	341	280	403	250	241	150
Haifa	159	99	95	56	–	–	69	43	210	130
Hebron	35	22	97	60	194	120	186	116	59	31
Jericho	39	24	101	63	148	92	118	73	117	73
Jerusalem	–	–	62	39	159	99	157	97	84	52
Metulla	221	137	196	122	121	75	65	40	301	187
Mezada (Masada)	109	66	169	104	261	161	183	113	64	39
Nazareth	157	97	102	63	35	22	29	18	217	135
Netanya	93	58	29	18	66	41	103	64	144	89
Rehovot	53	33	24	15	121	75	158	98	83	52
Rosh Haniqra	201	125	137	85	42	26	76	47	252	157
Tel Aviv	62	39	–	–	95	59	132	82	113	70
Tiberias	157	97	132	82	69	43	–	–	236	147
Zefat (Safed)	192	120	168	104	72	45	36	22	272	169

Fig. 5. Road distances.

Ben Gurion
If you land at Ben Gurion airport you have several possibilities. There is a regular flow of buses to both Jerusalem and Tel Aviv, as well as to Haifa and Be'er Sheva. If you intend to go to **Tel Aviv** take Egged bus no. 475 which runs every 20 minutes between 0505 and 2315 Sunday to Thursday; 0505 and 1635 on Friday; 1835 and 2315 on Saturday. You can also take United Tour shuttle bus no. 222 which runs hourly between 0400 and 2400 to Tel Aviv and stops at various places on the way. You can also take the El Al airline bus which goes to the airport terminal located in Arlosoroff Street in Tel Aviv. Remember that Arlosoroff Street is not very close to the centre of town and departure from the airport depends on El Al arrivals.

If you want to get to **Jerusalem** you can take one of the following Egged buses: 423, 425, 428, 945 or 947 to Jerusalem's central bus station. Most of these buses begin to run at 0600. Alternatively you can take United Tours bus no. 111 which departs hourly and stops at various places on the way. None of these stops are very convenient for the Old City or East Jerusalem.

Sherut
Another alternative for Jerusalem is to take a **sherut**, which is a shared taxi service. The airport service is Nesher Tours Taxi which will take you, as well as each of the other passengers, right to the door anywhere within the Jerusalem city limits.

Taxi
Another alternative for travel from the airport to your final destination is by taxi ('Special'). You will probably be approached by people offering to drive you to your destination. However, it is better to take a taxi from the taxi station which is located very close to the terminal. Most fares are posted on a massive sign and you should check this carefully before getting into the cab. There are two rates – daytime is applicable from 0530 to 2100 and night time from 2101 to 0529.

Bus to Haifa
The bus from Ben Gurion airport to Haifa, which is about one and a half hours away, leaves approximately every 20 minutes between 0700 and 1800.

TRAVELLING AROUND IN ISRAEL

Travelling in Israel is easy, roads are good and distances are relatively short (see Figure 5). It will take you about 90 minutes to cross Israel from the Mediterranean Sea (in the west) to the Dead Sea (in the east). Jerusalem is less than an hour's drive from Tel Aviv and a trip from Metulla, which is up in the far north, to Eilat at Israel's very southern tip might take you about nine hours.

You have several possibilities for travelling around in Israel, including domestic air flights, buses, trains, taxis, sheruts, hitch-hiking and cycling.

Travelling by air – domestic flights

Arkia, Israel's domestic airline, operates scheduled flights from the following locations:

Jerusalem to Tel Aviv, Haifa, Rosh Pina and Eilat
Tel Aviv to Jerusalem, Rosh Pina, Eilat and Mezada (Masada)
Haifa to Jerusalem, Tel Aviv, Eilat
Eilat to Jerusalem, Tel Aviv, Haifa
Mezada (Masada) to Tel Aviv

For enquiries contact one of the Arkia offices:

Eilat, 1001 Ha'kanyon Ha'adom. Tel: 07 6373388.
Haifa, 84 Ha'atzmaut Street. Tel: 04 8643371.
Jerusalem, Clal Centre, 97 Jaffa Road. Tel: 02 6255888.
Netanya, 10 Stemper Street. Tel: 09 843143.
Rosh Pina Airport. Tel: 06 936478.
Tel Aviv, Sde Dor Airport. Tel: 03 9602222/3333.

Snunit Aviation offers three daily flights in 19-seater aircraft between Tel Aviv and Ma'hanayyim airport (near Kiryat Shemona). Tel: 03 6993184.

Travelling by bus

Israel's bus network is dominated by Egged (the second largest bus company in the world, much ahead of London Transport) which operates about 4,000 buses on over 3,000 scheduled routes. Dan company provides a bus service in the Dan area – Tel Aviv and its environs. Generally Egged and Dan buses operate from about 0530 to about 1130; major routes go on until midnight. On busy inter-urban routes, mainly to and from Jerusalem, Tel Aviv and Haifa, the buses run almost continually through the day. The Israeli bus service is fast, very efficient and still relatively cheap.

• Remember that apart from Haifa, service is suspended between sunset on Friday and sunset on Saturday (the Shabath), as well as on religious holidays.

If you are a student you are eligible for discount fares on inter-urban bus routes on presentation of an international Student Card. In fact, there are quite a few special discounts; for example, 'Israbus' passes which are valid on all Egged bus lines, for periods of 7, 14, 21 and 30 days. Shop around for the best deal.

Useful telephone numbers
To find out about Egged's schedules, tickets and prices contact the following numbers:

Tel Aviv: 03 5375555.
Jerusalem: 02 5304555.
Haifa: 04 8549555.

Arab buses
In Nazareth, East Jerusalem and the Occupied Territories, small Arab companies are operating. The central bus station in East Jerusalem provides services to many destinations in Jerusalem and the West Bank. Prices are often cheaper than with Egged.

Travelling by train
The passenger network of the Israel State Railways is small (about 3 million passengers use it annually) and although cheaper than the buses it is not very convenient because of the location of many stations away from city and town centres.
   Israel Railways provides regular services between Tel Aviv and Herzliyya, Netanya, Hadera, Haifa, Akko and Nahariyya, as well as a daily train between Tel Aviv and Jerusalem, which follows a particularly beautiful scenic route. You can reserve a seat. All passenger trains include a buffet car. There are also a few trains which run from Rehovot to Tel Aviv via Ramla. Remember that there is no railway service on Shabath and major holidays.

Useful telephone numbers
To find out about schedules, tickets and prices for Israel Railways, contact the following numbers:

Tel Aviv: 03 5622200.
Haifa: 04 8303133.

Travelling by taxi

Most commonly, the service is called the **Sherut** and it operates on a fixed route at a fixed price. Rates are normally the same as buses and sometimes, because of competition, cheaper. A Sherut taxi drives off when it is full and you can get off anywhere along the way. After dropping off a passenger the Sherut picks up replacement passengers along the way. Sherut also operates on the Shabath and holidays and it is the major inter-city service when Egged is off the road.

Travelling by special taxis

You can get anywhere you wish using the 'Special' taxi and, unlike the Sherut, it will not pick up other passengers on the way. Beware, however, because drivers of Special taxis are notorious for overcharging. Ask the driver to use the meter or agree on the price before you get into the taxi. All urban taxis are equipped with meters and are required by law to operate them.

There are three distinct fare schedules, as indicated on the meter: (0) telephone surcharge to passenger pick-up point; (1) regular fare; and (2) fare + 25 per cent surcharge for night (2100 to 0530) and Shabath and holiday service. You may request a printed receipt after paying your fare.

Useful addresses and telephone numbers for complaints regarding taxi service
Tel Aviv and Central Region: 29 Yehuda Ha'yamit Street, 68134, Yaffo. Tel: 03 6821351.
Jerusalem and the South: 97 Jaffa Road (Box 867), 91008, Jerusalem. Tel: 02 6228550.
Haifa and the North: 121 Jaffa Road (Box 31097), Haifa. Tel: 04 8536711.

Travelling by car

Israel has a very good road system which makes it an ideal place to drive a car. In places like the Golan and The Negev, the buses do not cover so much ground and having your own car might save you a lot of time. For more information see Chapter 8.

Car rental
Most major international auto rental companies and several local ones have offices in Israel's major cities and at Ben Gurion Airport. Local care hire firms generally offer lower rates than the international companies. Eldan, in particular, stands out with good rates and

offices nationwide.

If you are planning to drive throughout the country use a company that has several offices in case you need a replacement car. Prices do vary considerably and shopping around is highly recommended. Check the *Jerusalem Post* and the free tourist magazines for special promotions. Most car rental companies require that drivers be over 23 years old and have a clean, valid driver's licence.

Useful addresses
Ben Gurion Airport: Budget, Tel: 03 9711504/5, Hertz. Tel: 03 9711165/6. Eldan, Tel: 03 9721027/8. Europcar, Tel: 03 9721097.
Tel Aviv: Avis, 12 Ha'masger. Tel: 03 6360000. Budget, 99 Ha'yarkon Street, Tel: 03 5227741. Eldan, 40 Ha'masger Street, Tel: 03 6394343. 112 Ha'yarkon Street, Tel: 03 5271166. Europcar, 126 Ha'yarkon Street, Tel: 03 5248181. Hertz, 10 Karlibach Street, Tel: 03 6841010.
Jerusalem: Budget, 24 King David Street. Tel: 02 6248902. Eldan, 24 King David Street. Tel: 02 6257555. Hertz, 18 King David Street. Tel: 02 6256334.

Cycling
If you are considering cycling around Israel, you must bear in mind the hot climate in much of the country, the frequent rainfall in certain areas at certain times and the steep hills. Hiring a bicycle locally for a few hours is not very common, but in Eilat, Tiberias and Jericho there are some places where you could hire bicycles.

Useful address
Eilat. Tel: 09 907171.

Hitch-hiking
Hitch-hiking is a common way for locals and visitors to get around. Soldiers are often seen hitch-hiking and Israelis are encouraged to give them lifts. The local signal is to point to the road with your index finger.

CHECKLIST

1. Is my passport still valid and with at least six months to run after my intended entry day to Israel?

2. How am I going to get to Israel; by air, land or sea? Do I know

how to get to my final destination in Israel?

3. Do I have a photocopy of the important pages of my passport and other documents?

4. Am I going to arrive at the weekend and have I got enough money to survive until banks are opened on Sunday?

CASE STUDIES – AN INTRODUCTION

We will be following three people who are about to go to Israel and intend to spend some time in the country doing different things. We will watch how they cope with difficulties and try to learn from their experiences. **John** will spend a year in a small Kibbutz in southern Israel where he will also study Hebrew. **Clair** will study at the Hebrew University, Jerusalem, and work in various part-time jobs. **Jill** will rent a flat in Tel Aviv and will work as an au pair in Herzeliyya before moving to work in the Israeli tourist industry in Eilat.

John Taylor, social worker

John is 38, single and lives in North London. He has decided to take a year off from work to visit Israel. John wishes to spend most of the year doing voluntary work on a Kibbutz or a Moshav. He also considers the possibility of helping with archaeological digs. But before doing that, he wants to travel a bit in Israel and most importantly take a Hebrew course. John, a most organised person, intends to organise everything while he is still in Britain.

Clair Wright, a student

Clair is 22 and lives in Northampton. She has just completed her BA in History and now intends to study at an Israeli University. Her parents are willing to pay the fees and help Clair with some expenses. Clair wishes to study in Jerusalem and she has already enrolled with the Department of History at the Hebrew University, Jerusalem. She also tries to get a place in Idelson, which is the Student Hall just five minutes walk from the University.

Jill Brown, hotel manager

Jill aged 25 was made redundant 18 months ago. She has now decided to go to Israel and find a job first in the area of Tel Aviv and then in the tourist industry in Eilat. Jill has visited Israel before and can speak some Hebrew. She loves the weather and gets on well with the Israelis. She takes with her some letters of recommendation and has prepared her Curriculum Vitae which she hopes may be helpful when she hunts for a job.

3
Knowing the Israelis

Meeting the Israelis in Israel can be quite a shock for you. You will very soon find out, for example, that you belong to a tiny minority who queue to get on a bus, while the natives are all jumping the queue. You will also realise (especially if you come from Britain) that one of the most dangerous places to cross a busy street in Israel is a Zebra crossing. But do not worry; soon you will get used to it all and you will behave (almost) as the Israelis do (otherwise you are likely to be waiting to get on a bus for ever or, God forbid, be knocked down by a car while crossing a busy street).

To shorten the 'cultural shock' (*Helem Ta'rbuti* in Hebrew) which you are likely to experience at the beginning of your visit, you need to try and understand the Israeli code of behaviour, manners and values.

VISITING A FAMILY

Israel is a place where you might find yourself talking to someone you have never met before and [s]he will tell you the story of his or her divorce within two minutes of meeting. But there are more conventional ways of meeting the Israelis and getting to know them.

Under the Ministry of Tourism's programme 'Meet the Israeli in his Home' you can meet an Israeli family in their own home. You can arrange a visit of this kind through any tourist information office and it usually takes up to 48 hours to arrange. You will be asked to give some details regarding your profession, hobbies and so on, so that you can be matched for common interests with the family you meet. Visits to an Israeli family can also be arranged through the **Voluntary Tourist Service** at:

Jerusalem, Jaffa Gate. Tel: 02 288140.
Haifa, 10 Ahad Ha'am Street. Tel: 04 8671645.
Nahariyya, 18 Sokolov Street. Tel: 04 9920135.

You can arrange to spend a Friday evening Shabath meal with an ultra-orthodox family. Do it through a tourist information centre, or at the Western Wall in Jerusalem. If you are invited to an Orthodox family try to be sensitive to their traditions by being suitably dressed (no shorts, no sleeveless dress and take a *Kipa* with you). If you bring a present to your religious hosts which is food or drink, make sure that it is *Kosher* (*Glant Kosher* is even better though more expensive). Ask the people in the shop for help and advice.

UNDERSTANDING MANNERS AND VALUES

In his lovely book *The Prophet Motive: Israel Today and Tomorrow*, which was written in 1969, George Mikes, a Hungarian Jew, summed up Israeli manners:

> Israeli manners [are] just as bad as ever before. Israelis keep teaching you your own business. God knows everything but the Israelis know everything better; they cannot bear to be wrong in anything. When you make a remark, they will interrupt you with 'of course, of course, of course...' meaning how silly it is to state the obvious at great length. Or cut you short with 'Ok, Ok, Ok' – meaning more or less the same. If they cannot butt in, they make faces, showing that they have already got the point and there is no need for you to go on nattering. They are quick witted and always up to conclusions.

While Mikes' description of Israeli manners is perfect, his conclusion (remember it was written in 1969), which is that 'politeness is slowly gaining ground' in Israel, is utterly flawed. Politeness has never been, and is still not, an Israeli strength. Israelis will say 'pass me the sugar' rarely using the word 'please'.

You will find Israelis straightforward, often sharp (native Israelis are known as *Sabras* which is a prickly cactus which is sweet on the inside) and impatient (the hot weather?). In situations which call for politely saying 'wait a minute' or 'please hold on', many Israelis just refrain from saying anything and instead raise their hand and purse their fingers together. This means '[please] hold on', or 'just a minute [please].

You in their eyes
Israelis usually love foreigners. They consider the English to be honest, polite and respectful. Some Israelis, especially of the older generation, know the British quite well from the years of the British

presence in Palestine (1919–1948).

If you are Scottish you will perhaps be surprised to find out that you are the principal hero of many Israeli jokes in almost all of which you are playing the role of the miser. Having said that, the only thing most Israelis are likely to know about you is that as a Scot you wear checked skirts and play a noisy instrument which is called *Hemet Halilim* in Hebrew. If you are Welsh expect to be considered English, and if you are Irish, the only thing most Israelis will know is that many bombs go off in your country.

Recognising social differences
The class system is basically non-existent in Israel. Israel is a young society and the fact that all serve in the army blurs all boundaries between potential different classes. It is just normal that someone coming from a poor family is the commander of someone else coming from a rich well-educated family. There are some slight differences in the Israeli dialect which do not show, however, that you are from a different class but mainly that you come from a different city. While a Tel Avivian would say, for example, *Mataim*, meaning two hundreds, a Jerusalem-born Israeli would say *Ma'ataim*.

The way they talk
Israelis use a range of expansive hand gestures when they talk; they touch whoever they are talking to and often raise their voice especially when someone else cuts them short. Israelis have in their vocabulary several unofficial words which reflect, perhaps more than anything else, their culture, service in the army and way of life.

- *Yallah* is a widely used Arabic word which can mean anything from 'Let's go' to 'come on' or 'move'. *Ya'allah* (pronounced slightly differently) can also be an expression of amazement: '*Ya'allah*, look at this beautiful girl!' It can also signify the Israeli seal of approval on a difficult business transaction: '*Yallah*, let's shake hands and seal this deal.' *Yallah* is also used to conclude a telephone conversation: '*Yallah*, bye then'.

- Another widely used word is the Yiddish *Nu*, meaning 1,000 different things. It can be a word of great impatience: '*Nu*, get away'. Or it can simply mean 'well' – '*Nu*, how are you?'

- Another very common expression, used by religious and non-religious alike, is *Ba'ruch Ha'shem* meaning 'Blessed is God'. To the question 'how are you?' a typical Israeli answer (even by a non-religious person) is '*Ba'ruch Ha'shem*' meaning 'all is well'.

Being a foreigner in Israel: some do's and dont's

• Avoid smoking in public on the Shabath (Friday night and Saturday) and remember that smoking is banned in the public rooms of hotels on these days. Smoking is not allowed on buses and in cinemas and theatres.

• When visiting churches, synagogues or mosques you should be suitably dressed; no shorts, no sleeveless dresses, or low necklines. Women must also cover their heads in mosques. In or near religious sites women should wear knee-length skirts and have blouses with sleeves of elbow length.

• When visiting a mosque remove your shoes before entering.

• In a synagogue, at the Western Wall, at the Yad Va'Shem Holocaust Memorial, or at funerals, men and boys (aged 13 and above) are expected to wear a *kipa*, or in some manner cover their heads. At Yad Va'shem, at the Wall, and at most synagogues, head covering is provided for visitors. You can purchase a *kipa* in shops all over the country.

• It is against the law to photograph military bases in Israel.

• Talking about the army, in social circumstances, is perfectly all right.

• The law says that Israelis must carry their identity cards at all times. Keep your passport at hand – just in case.

FOOD AND DRINK

Israel has no national cuisine and the dishes on the Israeli menu are a mixture of Western European, Arab and North African food. This variety reflects the many dimensions of Israeli society. You can eat well in Israel if you are willing to pay a lot; but you can also eat well and cheaply if you stick to the junk food, which is not bad at all, especially falafel, humous and shwarma.

Understanding the Kosher rules

Kosher food is food prepared in accordance with Jewish dietary laws. Meat of carnivorous animals and certain species of fish are banned, for example, eels. Only fish that have at least one fin and easily removable scales are allowed.

Animals that chew the cud and which have wholly cloven hooves are allowed, as well as chicken and turkey, but not birds of prey. Honey is allowed despite the bee's status as a forbidden insect.

The laws of Kashrut stipulate that the slaughter must be carried out by a licensed *Shoet*. The rule that the meat of an animal must not be boiled in the milk of its mother is interpreted by Orthodox Jews to mean that they cannot cook or eat meat and milk (including all dairy products) together. Five hours must be allowed between eating meat and drinking or eating dairy products. In order to ensure that meat is not eaten with milk, Jews keep separate utensils, dishes and cutlery, store them separately and wash them in separate sinks. Foods which are neither milk nor meat are known as *Parve* and may be eaten together with milk or meat.

Meals

Breakfast in Israel is made of eggs, vegetables, cheese and bread, coffee or tea. For lunch and dinner the main course is usually meat or fish.

Israeli specialities

Pitta	A flat, rounded, slightly leavened bread
Falafel	A ball of ground chick peas and spices served on slices of pitta bread along with salad
Tahina	A paste made from sesame seeds with oil, lemon and garlic
Humous	Boiled chick peas pureed with garlic, oil and lemon juice; often served with pitta bread
Shishlik	Beef or lamb spiced and grilled on the spot
Cholent	A stew of beans, potatoes and meat usually prepared over Friday and eaten on Saturday
Burekas	Flaky pastries filled with cheese, potatoes, mushrooms or spinach
Gefilte fish	Pieces of fish rolled into balls and cooked

Hallah   A traditional Jewish twisted loaf eaten on the Shabath

Kebab   Small pieces of beef or mutton, spiced and grilled on
              the spot

Beverages
Israelis drink tap water, although lately many have begun to drink
mineral water. Many of the other soft drinks found in the West are
also available. You can buy fresh pressed fruit juices in kiosks and
restaurants (try the carrot juice).

Coffee and tea
The most popular drink in Israel is coffee, either black Turkish
coffee or Nescafé. Israelis also drink tea, which they prefer black, or
with lemon, or peppermint.

Alcohol
'Few Israelis drink anything stronger than beer' wrote Mikes in
1969, but things have definitely changed in the last twenty years or
so. Today Israelis, and in particular, the younger generation, do
drink (and surprisingly enough get drunk!). There is a good choice
of local brandies and liqueurs including Sabra (chocolate and
orange). Israeli beers are Macabee, and Gold Star.

CASE STUDIES

John meets an Israeli family
John has just arrived in Israel, well before the day he is due to go to
Kibbutz Retamim in the Negev (south Israel). He is in a state of
shock! To get to know the Israelis better, he decides to go and meet
an Israeli family at their home. He visits the tourist centre in
Jerusalem and asks to participate in the 'Meet the Israeli in his
home' scheme. He is asked to fill in a questionnaire so that he can be
matched with a family. He would like to meet a family which speaks
English and is interested in archaeology. A visit is arranged and
John goes to see the Goldsmiths. He does not know if they are
religious or not and to stay on the safe side he decides not to bring a
present which is a food. He buys a huge bunch of flowers which his
hosts love very much. A lively discussion follows and John, who is
invited to join the family for supper, stays very late.

Clair lives in a student hall in Jerusalem

Clair was lucky to get a place and is delighted. Her room-mate is Yael, from Tel Aviv, who will study politics in the next academic year. Idelson Hall where Clair lives is very close to the university so she can walk to lectures, the library or to the cheap restaurant at the university. The room is not big but it is very convenient. She has her bed, her own desk, shelves and a cupboard. She can cook for herself in the small kitchen which is used by ten other students; there is also a shared fridge where Clair can keep her food. She has already found some new friends, two of whom will study with her in the History department.

Jill learns to economise

Jill is staying temporarily in a hostel in Ben Yehuda Street in Tel Aviv. She has not found a job yet and her plan is first to find a flat. In order not to spend too much money, Jill buys food in supermarkets and lives on Israeli junk food, mainly falafel.

4
Learning Hebrew

Hebrew is the official language of Israel along with Arabic. English, the most common second language, is a mandatory subject at school.

Hebrew is a very successful experiment in reviving a long-dead language and turning it into one in daily use. The man who revived Hebrew was Eliezer Ben-Yehuda, who lived from 1858 to 1922 and while in Palestine devoted his life to turning biblical Hebrew into a daily-spoken language.

Hebrew script is written from right to left and is composed of consonents only. A system of vowel signs – dots and lines with the characters – helps the reader to properly pronounce words. (See Figure 6.)

Ivrit Safa Ka'sha (Hebrew is a difficult language) but it is not impossible to learn it and the better you know it the easier it will be for you to settle in Israel. So do try to learn some Hebrew before you go to Israel – you will never regret it.

STARTING BEFORE YOU GO

There are Hebrew courses at different levels which are run by private schools and, especially in London, by local authorities. Look in the local newspapers for openings and check in your local library.

Courses are also run by **The Jewish Agency for Israel**, Department of Jewish Education and Culture in Diaspora. Although the courses are designed for Jewish people, non-Jews can also join. Courses are at all levels and are taught by Israeli teachers. Fees are to cover expenses. For more information ring: Shoshana on (0181) 446 8109.

Alternatively you can buy a home study course or a good book and teach yourself. You can purchase home study courses and books in the big bookshops: WH Smith, Dillons, Waterstones. One recommended book is:

אꟷ	א	alef
	ב	bet
	ב	vet
	ג	gimel
	ד	dalet
	ה	he
	ו	vav
	ז	zain
	ח	ḥet
	ט	tet
	י	yod
	כ	kaf
	כ, ך	khaf
	ל	lamed
	מ, ם	mem
	נ, ן	nun
	ס	samekh
	ע	ain
	פ	pe
	פ, ף	fe
	צ, ץ	tzadi
	ק	kof
	ר	resh
	שׁ	shin
	שׂ	sin
	ת	tav

Fig. 6. The Hebrew alphabet.

• Edna Amir Coffin, *Encounters in Modern Hebrew: Levels 1 & 2*
(University of Michigan Press, 1995). The book is in three
volumes and is designed to introduce English-speaking students
to modern Hebrew.

STUDYING HEBREW IN ISRAEL

Finding a place to learn Hebrew in Israel is neither easy nor cheap.
Most *Ulpanim* (language schools) cater for new Jewish immigrants
and because many Jews are still coming to the country every year,
there are only a few places for non-Jews. But this does not mean that
it is impossible to find an Ulpan.
Try in Jerusalem where prices are a bit cheaper. Contact the
Ulpan Office, Division of Adult Education, Beir Ha'am, 11 Betzalel
Street, Jerusalem 94591. Tel: 02 6254157. Also try the following:

1. YMHA (Hebrew Youth Centre), 105 Herzog Street, Jerusalem.
   Tel: 02 789441 or 02 780442.
2. Mo'adon Ha'ole, 9 Alkalay Street, Jerusalem. Tel: 02 5633718.
3. Beit Mitchell, 17 Straus Street, Jerusalem. Tel: 02 6257950.

You can also look in the local newspaper for openings and consider
the possibility of putting your own adverts to teach English in return
for someone teaching you Hebrew. You could put your ads on the
noticeboards at one of the universities or colleges where there are
Israeli students who are desperate to find someone who could teach
them English.

Ulpan Akiva Netanya
Although a bit expensive, this is one of the best schools to learn
Hebrew in Israel, and one where you are likely to get a place. Ulpan
Akiva is an independent international residential Hebrew study
centre located at the Green Beach Hotel in Netanya. The Ulpan,
which also runs Arabic courses, aims not only to teach you the
language but also to bring you closer to Israeli society by organising
lectures about Jewish/Israeli matters.
   The Ulpan is open to everybody aged 18 and over, including
families with children (who must be over 12 years of age), regardless
of social and cultural background, nationality, faith and status in
Israel (tourists, temporary residents, immigrants, etc.).

Choosing a course

The most comprehensive course offered by Ulpan Akiva is the **Complete Programme of Modern Hebrew** which is between 16 and 20 weeks. It is for those who wish to acquire a general knowledge of Hebrew, as well as those who already have some knowledge of the language. Graduates of this course receive an official certificate of the Israeli Department of Adult Education, Ministry of Education and Culture.

The other courses on offer are of 12 weeks (covering part of the above course), 8 weeks and 24 days, which aim to provide you with the ability to use a basic everyday vocabulary of around 600 words and a general introduction to reading and writing.

Your first day at Ulpan Akiva

On the first morning between 0830 and 1000 you will finalise your registration, take the class-placement test and then be assigned to your room where you will meet your teacher and classmates. There is also a social get-together after supper.

Classes and non-classes hours

Classes are run from Sunday to Friday in the morning and afternoon. When classes are not in session you have time for:

• individual study, tutoring and conversational practice

• optional programme which may include lectures on Jewish history and Zionism

• special events which are planned to familiarise you with Jewish heritage, the country and the people including trips, visits and concerts.

Fees

The fees include full board in a modest room at the Green Beach Hotel, tuition, use of hotel facilities, sports facilities, tennis, swimming pool. Fees do not, however include textbooks, special events, travelling and medical insurance or visa.

Fees depend on the season, the length of course you intend to take and the number of people with whom you are willing to share a room (the greater the number the cheaper the price you will have to pay).

For example: taking the Complete Programme of Modern Hebrew between 10 September 1995 and 24 January 1996 would have cost you, if you were *not* sharing a room, about £9,516. The same course but a room shared with another person would have cost you about £6,450. Sharing a room with three other people would have cost you about £4,836.

Registering

You can ask for further information and an application form by writing to: Ulpan Akiva, PO Box 6086, 42160 Netanya, Israel. Tel: 09 352312.

If you decide to take the course you will be asked to send:

- a completed application form
- medical certificate from your GP
- two letters of recommendation
- three passport-size photographs
- Curriculum Vitae in your own handwriting
- advance payment equivalent of $1,000.

Travelling to the Ulpan

You will have to get to the Ulpan by yourself.

Buses

From Tel Aviv central station take bus express 605 or regular bus 601 to the central bus station (*Tachana Merkazit*), Netanya. From there take bus no. 7 (which leaves approximately 30 minutes from stand 18 just outside the central bus station) to Green Beach Hotel and Ulpan Akiva.

Taxis

If you are coming from Tel Aviv, Haifa or Jerusalem it is recommended that you arrive at Netanya by bus and from there, if you wish, take a 'Special'.

From the airport

Take a bus to the central bus station at Netanya and from there as above.

LANGUAGE COURSE WITH WORK ON A KIBBUTZ

The working Hebrew scheme

The purpose of this programme is to provide you with the opportunity to work on a Kibbutz and gain a fair knowledge of conversational Hebrew and the ability to read simple texts. You will be working a 36-hour week and have an additional 12 hours of Hebrew lessons which will be given by qualified teachers. The division of work and study will depend on the daily needs of the Kibbutz. The course is three months long and may also include occasional lectures. For more details contact:

Kibbutz Representatives: 1A Accommodation Road, London NW11. Tel: (0181) 458 9235.

Ulpan – Hebrew language course

The Kibbutz Ulpan, for students who live and work on a Kibbutz, is primarily for those thinking of becoming candidates for membership and for Jewish applicants, but non-Jews can also try to get onto the course through the Kibbutz representatives. The programme includes four hours study and four hours work, and students are expected to devote time each day for homework. Some aspects of Jewish history and current events will be covered. You must be aged between 17½ and 35; single or a couple without children. For more details contact the Kibbutz Representatives at the above address.

CASE STUDIES

John learns the language

John Taylor is taking a 24-day course in Hebrew at Ulpan Akiva, Netanya. To save some money he has decided to share a room with three other people, two from the UK and one from Spain. John has already met his teacher and schoolmates and is now settling into his new room at the Beach Hotel. He hopes that by the end of the course he will be able to talk a little and have a basic everyday vocabulary and read a bit. After the course John is going to work on Kibbutz Retamim.

Clair and her room mate Yael strike a deal

Yael will teach Clair some words in Hebrew and, in return, Clair will help Yael with English. Today Clair had her first lesson and she now knows five words in Hebrew: Ken (Yes); Lo (No); Bevakasha (Please); Toda (Thank you); Toda Raba (Thank you very much). She also knows one very important sentence: Ani Lo Medaberet Ivit, meaning: I don't speak Hebrew.

Jill has decided to DIY

Though she knows some words in Hebrew Jill decided to learn some more. She went to Allenby and Dizingoff streets in Tel Aviv, where there are quite a few book shops and she found a good home study course of Hebrew. She will learn the language in her free time.

DISCUSSION POINTS

1. Shop around before going to Israel and see if you can find a home study course in Hebrew which suits you.

2. Compare the Hebrew course of Ulpan Akiva Netanya, the language course with work on the Kibbutz and any other Hebrew course you have heard of, and decide which one suits you best.

3. When you have decided which course suits you, contact the place and register. Try to do that even before leaving Britain.

5
Finding Accommodation

The decision about where you live and whether your rent or buy a flat or house depends on your specific circumstances. If you are a student in Tel Aviv you are likely to rent or buy in the Tel Aviv area; if you work in Be'er Sheva you are unlikely to buy in Haifa. Your budget is, of course, another very important consideration. If you are a typical poor student with a limited budget you are more than likely to opt for the cheaper option which is a rented, shared flat.

Generally speaking, accommodation is much more expensive in the big cities with Tel Aviv and Jerusalem at the top of the league. The rule of thumb is that the further you go from the centre of town the cheaper accommodation becomes.

RENTING A PLACE

Even if you intend to buy it is very likely that you will first live in rented accommodation. You can either share a flat with other people or rent your own place and later decide whether or not you wish to share it with other people.

Hunting for a flat

If you wish to share a rented flat the best thing to do is to look on the noticeboards in universities and colleges. Even if you do not read Hebrew you can easily spot these offers by the typical cuttings at the bottom of the notes which carry a telephone number.

You can also look at the ads in your local or national papers. Ask a friend to help you look through the ads in the daily *Ma'ariv* and *Yediot Ahronot*, especially on Tuesdays and Fridays, as well as at supplements such as *Arim*.

A more expensive way of hunting for a flat is to place your own ads. Ring your local newspaper for more details or use the following telephone numbers if you wish to advertise in a national newspaper:

Dahaf. Tel: 02 6256335 (takes ads for all the national newspapers).
The Jerusalem Post. Tel: 02 5315666.
Yediot Ahronot. Tel: 03 6972222.
Ha'aretz. Tel: 03 9648750.
Ma'ariv. Tel: 03 5632111.

Making inquiries

Once you have the telephone number of a flat which might suit you, the next step is to telephone to find out more information. Do not hesitate to ask the lender if [s]he speaks English. Many do and will be more than happy to use (and perhaps improve) their language skills. Ask all your questions and try to find out everything you want to know about the potential flat. The following **checklist** might help you with inquiries:

• How many rooms are there in the flat?

• What floor is the flat on and is there a lift? (You pay more money for a flat with a lift.)

• Is the flat furnished? What about oven, microwave, fridge, TV, washing machine?

• How many people live in the flat?

• Is there a policy on smoking?

• How much is the *Arnona* (council tax which is high in certain areas; for example, in the Givathaim suburb of Tel Aviv)?

• How much is the rent?

• Does the price include all bills and if not what should you expect to pay for gas, electricity and so on?

If you are satisfied with the answers then your next stage is to arrange a visit. Remember that if you are going to share a flat you want to see not only where your potential room is, but also who the potential partners are. Try to develop a conversation and discover who the sharers are, what they are doing and so on. If, for example they are all opera singers who spend the whole day practising at home then maybe this flat is not for you (or maybe it is!).

Signing the contract

If you join a flat where other people are already living you will probably have to sign an informal agreement with the others. However, if you are renting a flat for yourself, or are the first to rent and will only later share the flat with other people, then you will have to sign a contract with the landlord.

Take a friend who reads Hebrew, as contracts are often very complicated documents. Most renting contracts are standard and you therefore need to pay extra attention to any changes made to the original document. The landlord might ask you to pay in advance for three or six months or even a year; this is negotiable and if you wish to pay monthly then all you have to do is to insist.

The contract will include provisions about termination of the contract and compensation if either side breach the contract. You will probably be asked to leave a deposit (usually one month's rent) or a *Shetar Itchaivut* which you can purchase at the Post Office for £2 or so and which should be signed by two people. Most landlords have now abandoned this practice which is anyway not very practical because the landlord can do nothing with the document unless he takes you to court.

Some landlords add a list of the flat's contents. Make sure that it says in the contract that the landlord is to pay for repairing household equipment such as washing machine and fridge.

Using an agent

This is the easiest option but it has its drawbacks. An agent can easily find a flat for you but effectively what an agent does is what you can do (maybe with the help of an Israeli friend) – look at the ads of your local and national papers.

An agent can be expensive, charging you between half and a full month's rent for his or her services. If you do decide to use an agent, make sure that you agree *in advance* on the fee. Ask if the fee includes VAT which is now 17 per cent.

BUYING A PLACE

The same old story: it is expensive to buy in the big cities and close to the centre and much cheaper in small towns and far from the centre. But you have to remember that commuting takes time and costs money.

A comparison between Britain and Israel is interesting. In Britain, especially in the cities, buying is relatively cheap but renting is expensive. In Israel, buying is very expensive and renting relatively cheap.

Unlike Britain where most flats and houses are bought through agencies, in Israel buying a place is usually through advertisements. Look in your local newspaper and also in the big national newspapers *Ma'ariv, Yediot Ahronot*, and also *Ha'aretz* and *The Jerusalem Post* especially on Tuesdays and Fridays. You will find in some of these newspapers tables which show the number of rooms, the floor, the name of the street and the price which is usually quoted in American dollars.

Making inquiries
Ring the number and, again, do not hesitate to ask the person on the other end of the telephone if s[he] speaks English. You want to be able to have all the information about the flat before arranging a visit. The following **checklist** might help you in your inquiries:

• the number of rooms and their size

• the direction of the rooms (south = hot in summer; north = cooler)

• the floor and whether there is a lift

• the *arnona* (council tax) in the area

• the approximate time it will take from signing of contract and departure of previous occupant

• schools in the area: their standard

• what public transport is available

• what shops and supermarkets are nearby

• parking place (more expensive if there is a parking place, but it does save a lot of trouble especially in big cities)

• the price and is it negotiable.

If you are satisfied with the answers, ask to arrange a visit. Try to come during the day so you can spot all the defects, look out of the windows and listen to potential noises (busy road, for example). Pay attention to detail and don't hesitate to go back for a second or even third look. Do take notes – it is easy to forget things and to confuse two properties. You need to ignore the decor and furnishing – try to picture the property empty. If you are not sure about the price you can ask to have a survey. You will have to pay for it (you can find surveying services in the *Yellow Pages*).

Signing the contract

When you are confident that you have found the right place for you then you can make a formal offer. But first try to ask for a reduction in the price.

You will need a solicitor to help with the arrangements. Your solicitor's main job will be conveyancing – the legal transfer of ownership of your new home. You will have to pay a purchase tax (*Mas Keniya* in Hebrew).

The way to find a solicitor is by word-of-mouth or *Yellow Pages*; if you buy through an estate agency they can give you the name of a solicitor. A solicitor will usually charge between 0.5 and 2 per cent (+ VAT) of the price of the flat. You will have to discuss with your solicitor all the details regarding payments, taxes and transfer of the flat to your name.

Using an agent

Using an agent is the easiest, though not the cheapest, way of buying a place in Israel. An agent will take a commission of between 1 and 2 per cent (+ VAT) which comes on top of the commission which you pay for a solicitor and other taxes. The advantage of an agent however, is that [s]he saves you the hassle of looking at the ads, and can recommend you a solicitor to work with you. Do remember to agree on the commission *before* beginning to work with an estate agent.

You want to register with a number of different estate agents and visit a lot of properties. If you decide to take this option use one of the well-established estate agents like Anglo-Saxon, Diur 2000.

SETTLING INTO YOUR HOME

Britain–Israel: spot the differences

The Israeli style is very different from the British. First, in most flats you will find no wall-to-wall carpet. Instead the floor is a stone floor which makes it much easier to clean (the Israeli style of floor-cleaning is pouring a bucket of water over it, which not only cleans but it also cools the place in the hot summer). Only a few places are decorated with wallpaper; instead most Israelis paint on the wall itself. Washing machines are not in the kitchen (God forbid!) but in the bathroom and there is probably no flat in Israel without a good shower (which means that the bath is mostly used for putting the fish in when you clean the aquarium). In Israel there are no separate taps for hot and cold water; instead one tap is in use which mixes hot and cold water.

In every Israeli flat you will probably find sliding doors which does save a lot of space. Only a few flats have central heating; instead heating is either by gas or by electricity. Unlike in Britain, Israelis put their surnames on the name-plate and often the names of all the family not forgetting, of course, the dog.

Furnishing and buying household equipment

If you are renting the flat it will probably be furnished. If buying you will probably have to furnish it yourself (in most places there is a built-in kitchen). You could also ask the previous tenants if they want to sell their furniture or part of it.

It is not very common to buy second-hand furniture in Israel; there are no charity shops, no jumble sales and no car boot sales. If you insist on buying second-hand you should go to **Shuk Ha'pishpeshim** in Jaffa. If you see something you want to buy do not show too much enthusiasm and try to negotiate the price. New furniture can be bought in many shops in most towns and cities.

You will probably find it necessary to buy a washing machine since there are only a few launderettes. You can buy a washing machine through **Ampa** which is the biggest importer of electric household machines. Shop around because buying through an agent can be much cheaper.

You can buy new household equipment such as cutlery and crockery in many shops in your town or city. For good bargains go to **Shuk Ha'Carmel** in Tel Aviv or visit shops in South Tel Aviv. For more details see Chapter 8.

PAYING YOUR BILLS

Whether you rent or buy property you will have to pay for the use of water (the bill also inlcudes council tax – called *Arnona*), electricity and gas (if you use gas). You can pay these bills at any post office, bank or by direct debit.

When you receive a bill always make sure that your name and

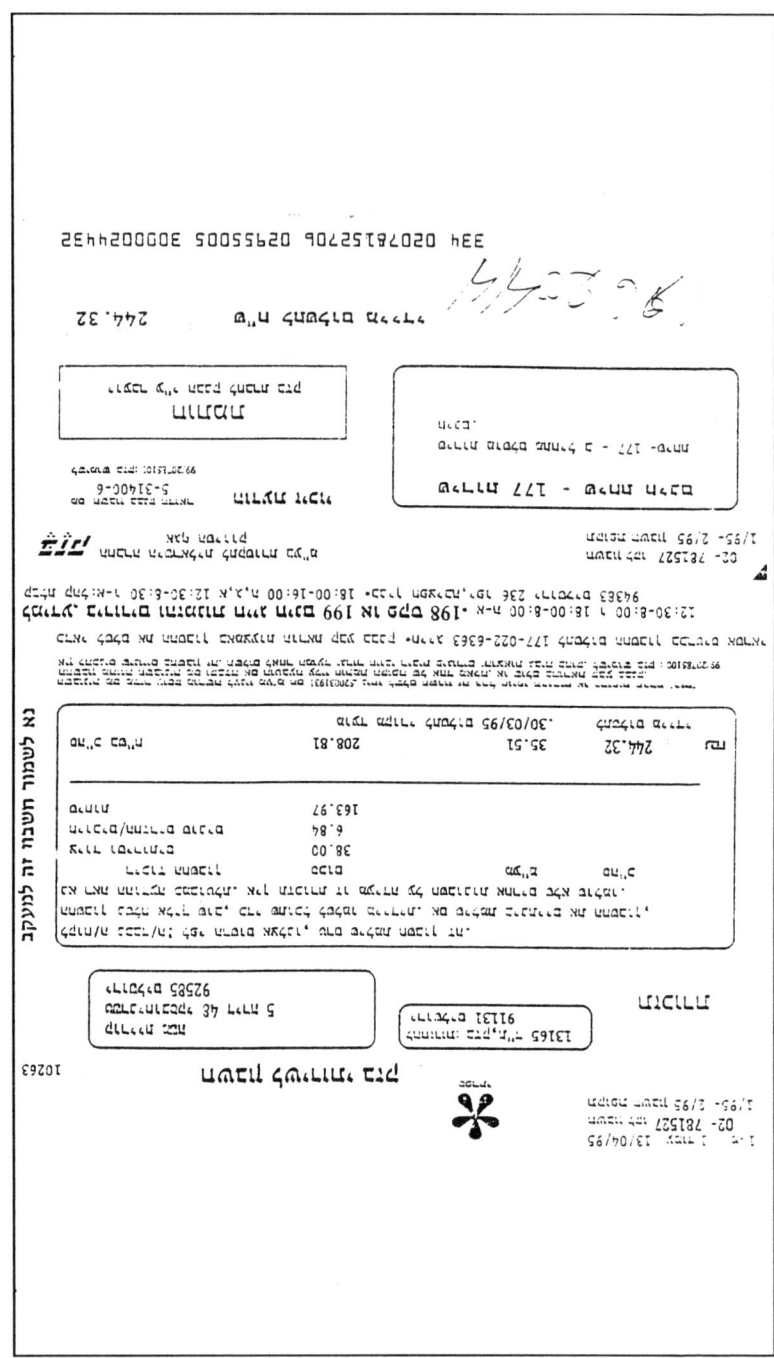

Fig. 7. Example of a telephone bill.

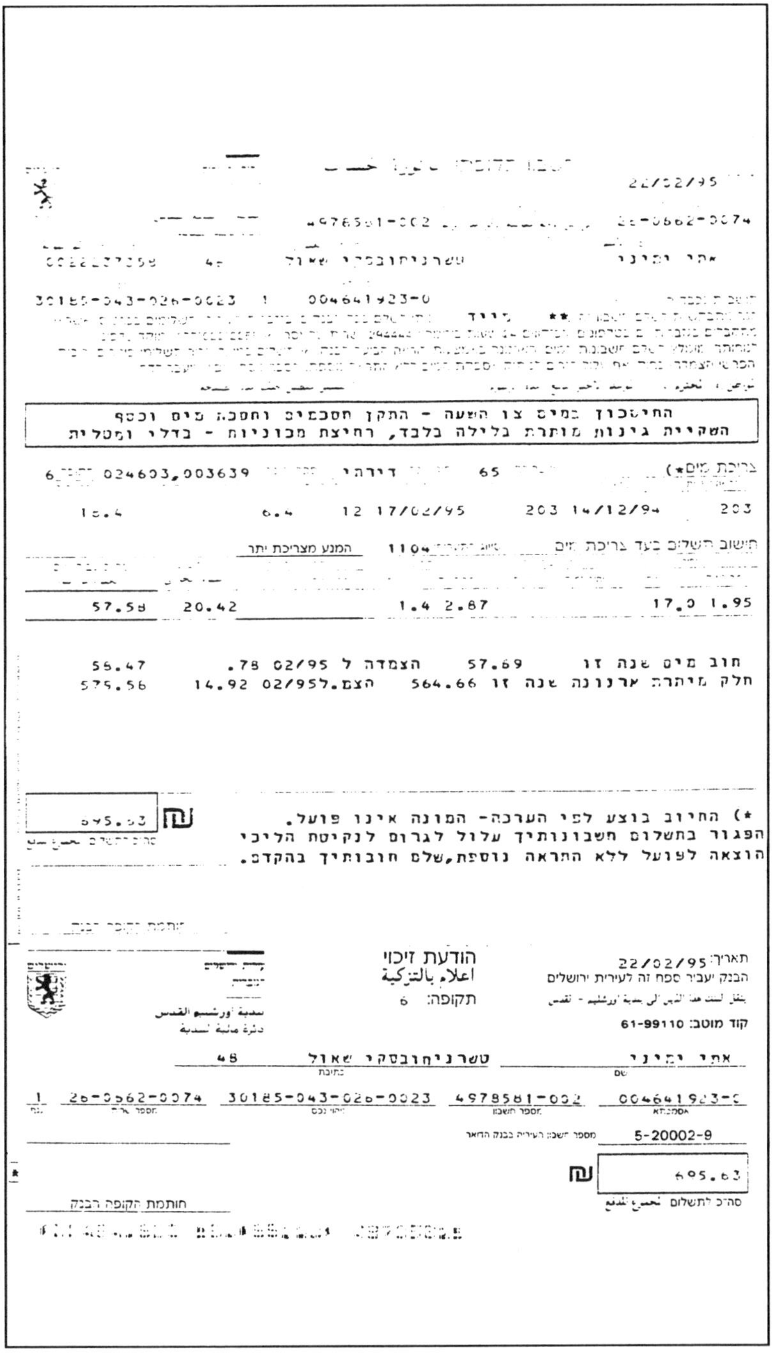

22/02/95

497851-002 26-0662-0074

0022237358 48 טשרניחובסקי שאול אתי ימיני

30185-043-026-0023 1 004641923-0

החיסכון במים צו השעה - התקן חסכמים וחסכה מים וכסף
השקיית גינות מותרת בלילה בלבד, רחיצת מכוניות - בדלי ומטלית

6 024603,003639 דירתי 65 צריכת מים*)

15.4 6.4 12 17/02/95 203 14/12/94 203

חישוב תשלום בעד צריכת מים 1104 המנע מצריכת יתר

57.58 20.42 1.4 2.87 17.0 1.95

חוב מים שנה זו 57.69 הצמדה ל 02/95 .78 56.47
חלק מיתרה ארנונה שנה זו 564.66 הצמ.02/957 14.92 575.56

*) החיוב בוצע לפי הערכה- המונה אינו פועל.
הפגור בתשלום חשבונותיך עלול לגרום לנקיטת הליכי
הוצאה לפועל ללא התראה נוספת,שלם חובותיך בהקדם.

595.63

הודעת זיכוי
اعلام بالتزكية

תאריך: 22/02/95
הבנק יעביר ספח זה לעירית ירושלים

תקופה: 6

קוד מוטב: 61-99110

אתי ימיני טשרניחובסקי שאול 48

שם כתובת

00464192З-0 4978581-002 30185-043-026-0023 26-0562-0074 1

אסמכתא מספר חשבון זיהוי נכס מספר ארנונה

מספר חשבון העיריה בבנק הדואר 5-20002-9

695.63

סה"כ לתשלום

חותמת הקופה בבנק

Fig. 8. Example of a water bill.

address appear at the top of it just to make sure that you don't pay someone else's bill. You can use the telephone number which appears on the bill if you have any queries. Remember it is better to pay on time – fines are high in Israel and the supply of water, electricity and gas can be cut off if you fail to pay. (See Figures 7 and 8 for example bills.)

LEARNING SOME USEFUL WORDS

English	Hebrew
A flat	Di-ra
A house	Ba-it
To rent	Li-s-kor
To buy	Li-k-not
An ad	Mo-da-aa
How many rooms?	Kama Ha-da-rim?
The size of the rooms?	Ma Go-del Ha-Ha-da-rim?
Which floor is the flat?	Ei-zo Ko-ma Ha-dira?
Is there a lift?	Yesh Ma-a-lit?
How many tenants?	Kama Shu-ta-fim?
How much does it cost?	Kama ze-ole?
How much is the council tax?	Kama Ha-arnona?
When is it possible to view?	Ma-tai ef-shar li-r-ot?

CASE STUDIES

Jill is looking for a rented flat in Tel Aviv
She wants to share a flat with two or three students and she has already looked at some ads on the university noticeboard. She rings the telephone number and says in Hebrew: 'Ani Lo me-da-be-ret Iv-rit. Ha'im A-ta me-daber An-glit? (which means: I do not speak Hebrew do you speak English?) The man says: 'Of course I do' and so the discussion is in English. Jill asks all the information she needs, including the number of tenants, their occupation and the monthly rent and then she asks if she can visit and have a look. She will go there later in the week.

John is now staying in Tel Aviv before moving to the Kibbutz
He has just completed his Hebrew course, which he very much enjoyed, and he has two weeks to spend before going to work on the Kibbutz. John decided to stay for a while in Tel Aviv, but two weeks is a relatively short period of time to rent a flat and John decided to

stay in a hostel. He visited some hostels especially in Ben Yehuda Street and in the end found a lovely place in Ha'yarkon Street very close to the beach in Tel Aviv.

Clair has a bright idea

Why not spend the period of the Jewish festivals, when the University is closed, in Haifa? With the help of an Israeli friend she found a student who lives in the student halls in Haifa. They will swap rooms – Clair will move for two weeks to Haifa and the student from Haifa – Neomi – will move into Clair's room.

DISCUSSION POINTS

1. You wish to rent a flat. First try to decide where you want to live. Then the type of property you wish to rent, how much you can afford to pay and whether or not you want to share a flat with other people.

2. Having pinpointed the area in which you want to live and decided on the type of property you wish to rent, you now have to take the next step and ring to ask for more details regarding a flat. Before doing that, draw up a list of questions you wish to ask.

3. You wish to buy your own property. First decide where you want to live and which type of property (a flat or a house) you wish to buy. Then decide how much you can afford and whether you will look for your dream home using the help of an estate agency (or maybe do it yourself). In either case, draw up a list of the important things you want to look for when viewing a potential place.

6
Voluntary Work in Israel

There are several opportunities for voluntary work in Israel, ranging from work on the Kibbutz and Moshav to archaeological digs. There are also occasional jobs such as teaching in underdeveloped towns. You need to remember two very important things about voluntary work in Israel. First, you will be expected to commit yourself fully to the job and work very hard, sometimes in harsh weather conditions, while the incentive of a salary will not be there. Second, in all types of voluntary work you yourself will have to pay a certain amount of money in order to get to Israel and back, register and insure yourself and pay for visas.

Pros and cons of voluntary work

A volunteer is a person who offers unpaid help. Before you decide to become a volunteer look at the following list of pros and cons, add to it points which are relevant to your specific circumstances, and then see if you fit the bill.

Pros
- My work will contribute to society.

- As a volunteer I will do something which really interests me and contributes to my own satisfaction.

- As a volunteer I might be offered free, or very cheap, accommodation.

Cons
- As a volunteer I will not be paid, apart from some pocket money.

- I will have to commit myself fully to a minimum period of time and I might be tied to the same place and work for quite some time.

If you still want to go ahead and take a voluntary job, the next step is to choose from the three main types of voluntary work in Israel:

• work on a Kibbutz
• work on a Moshav
• work in archaeological excavations.

WORKING ON A KIBBUTZ

What is a Kibbutz?

A Kibbutz (*pl.* Kibbutzim) is a communal settlement in which work, income and property are shared by its members (known as *Kibbutzniks*), fulfilling the principle 'From each according to his ability, to each according to his needs.' Having said that, in the modern Kibbutz private property does exist, although it is limited to personal possessions.

Today 2.4 per cent of the Israeli population live in some 270 Kibbutzim. Kibbutz members generally work within their community in agriculture, light industry and the services, although some members do work outside the community in regional enterprises which belong to the Kibbutz or to the Kibbutz movement.

In the Kibbutz, the work co-ordinator organises the daily work according to the needs of the Kibbutz and each member's long-term work placement. The general assembly of the Kibbutz meets on a regular basis to make decisions, and committees handle education, housing, finance, health, production planning and culture. Most, though not all, Kibbutz posts are rotational. Children are raised communally but, unlike the practice of the past, they now live with their parents.

What will you do as a Kibbutz volunteer?

As a Kibbutz volunteer you will work alongside the Kibbutzniks in all sorts of work, including farming, gardening and industry. In addition, you will have to take your turn at helping with cooking, cleaning and laundry for the whole community. You will normally work eight hours a day six days a week, starting early in the summer to avoid the heat of the day. After work your free time is your own.

What will you get in return?

You will get free accommodation: usually a basic room shared with between two and four other volunteers. Male and female volunteers will sleep in separate rooms even if they arrive as a mixed couple.

You will also get free meals which you will take together with members of the Kibbutz in the communal dining-room. You will be allowed to use all the other facilities which are on the Kibbutz: swimming pool, library, and cultural events. Some Kibbutzim still give pocket money, which, is however, very little in expensive Israel; others give you tokens which you can use in the Kibbutz canteen.

Do you fit the bill?
These are the important points to remember before you decide whether voluntary work on a Kibbutz is for you:

● You should be between 18 and 32 and in good physical and mental health.

● You will be expected to work between six and eight hours a day, six days a week in agriculture, light industry or one of the services.

● You must be able to commit yourself for at least eight weeks.

● You will have to share a fairly basic room with between two and four other volunteers.

● You will be expected to conform with the regulations of the Kibbutz for as long as you are living there.

● Drugs are not allowed on the Kibbutz and negative behaviour resulting from drinking is unlikely to be acceptable.

If you still want to become a Kibbutz volunteer then it is recommended that you book a place in a Kibbutz while still in Britain. You should do so through the services of either the Kibbutz Representatives or Project 67.

Applying through the Kibbutz Representatives
Stage 1:   Contact the Kibbutz Representatives and ask for details and an application form.

Stage 2:   Send a completed application form to the **London Office** of the Kibbutz Representatives.

Stage 3:   Ring the Kibbutz Representatives and arrange an interview in London, Manchester or Glasgow.

• Remember: your place is not guaranteed until after a successful interview, or if you do not attend an interview, after a letter of confirmation.

Attending the interview
This will last for approximately one and a half hours, by which time you will have seen a film about Kibbutz volunteering, met other people who plan to go to a Kibbutz and had the opportunity to talk to a Kibbutz Representative who can answer your questions.

If you want to be interviewed in Manchester or Glasgow it is important that you mention it clearly in the application form, but again remember that the application should be sent to the London office. Applicants resident in Ireland, the Channel Islands or remote areas of Britain are not required to attend an interview. Just send the completed application form and say that you live in either of the above places.

Within ten days (approximately) you will receive an indication from the Representatives as to whether your application is successful.

Useful addresses
Kibbutz Representatives (London office), 1A Accommodation Road, London NW11 8ED. Tel: (0181) 458 9235. Or (Tel Aviv office) 18 Frischman Street, Tel Aviv. Tel: 03 5278874.
Manchester interview address, Peltours Ltd, 27–29 Church Street, Manchester M4 1QA.
Glasgow interview address, 222 Fenwick Road, Giffnock, Glasgow G46 6UE.

Following a successful interview, you can decide on your date of travel and whether you want to go with a group or individually.

Going with a group
If you join a group you will be invited for a group meeting approximately a week before departure. On the day you travel to Israel you will meet your group at Gatwick, Heathrow or Manchester airports. A representative of the Kibbutz will meet the group at Ben Gurion airport near Tel Aviv from where [s]he will take you to the Kibbutz where you are placed.

Going on your own
The only advantage of this is that you have more flexibility in choosing when to arrive in Israel. You will make your own

arrangements through the Representatives' travel desk and after landing in Israel you should go to the Representatives' office in Tel Aviv; they will place you in a Kibbutz. Placement occasionally takes more than one day in which case you will be responsible for your own accommodation (accommodation for the first night is included in the package).

Checking visa and passport requirements

See Chapter 1. Remember, if you hold a second passport or if you are not a British subject you should consult the Consular section of the Israeli Embassy. Do this before sending your forms or laying out any money.

Arranging insurance

Whilst on a Kibbutz you will receive free medical attention but the Kibbutz will not pay for expenses of hospitalization, personal accident or loss of luggage. That is why you need to take out an insurance policy specifically tailored for this scheme. This insurance is comprehensive and, as well as covering you for your Kibbutz working holiday, will cover you while travelling around Israel.

How much will it cost?

The Kibbutz Representatives' package price includes the following elements: return flights, UK and Israel airport taxes, and either overnight accommodation in Tel Aviv or transfer to the Kibbutz. In 1995, prices for an open or fixed return flight from Gatwick (charter) were between £272 and £312; from Heathrow (schedule) between £316 and £356. Insurance (compulsory) for four months was from £33, eight months from £44 and twelve months from £52. The pre-booking deposit was £50 paid when applying. A typical Kibbutz package in 1995 was approximately £335 including insurance.

Applying through Project 67

You can also apply for voluntary work on a Kibbutz through Project 67 which is a private organisation set up in 1967.

Stage 1:   Contact Project 67 and ask for details and an application form.

Stage 2:   Send back a completed application form together with a passport-size photo, a medical declaration and a deposit of £75 per person.

You will be sent a confirmation invoice which will advise you of the time of your briefing meeting which will be held in London approximately three weeks prior to your departure. Full payment is required eight weeks prior to departure, or at time of booking if less than eight weeks. You will also have to take out insurance which is arranged for you by the company.

No one will be waiting to meet you when you land in Israel, and you will have to go to Tel Aviv where you will probably stay overnight (included in the package deal) and call in at the Tel Aviv office the next day. From there you will be sent to a Kibbutz.

How much will it cost?

In 1996/7 prices for a fixed return of maximum six months were between £269 and £299. Open return of maximum twelve months was between £299 and £329. £10 airport tax was not included in the price. Travel insurance (compulsory) up to eight weeks was £45, up to three months £60, up to six months £85 and each additional month £22.

Useful addresses
UK office: Project 67, 10 Hatton Garden, London EC1N 8AH. Tel: (0171) 831 7626. Fax: (0171) 404 5588.
Israel office: Project 67, 94 Ben Yehuda Street, Tel Aviv. Tel: 03 5230140.

Applying in Israel

It is possible to apply for Kibbutz voluntary work while in Israel, although between June and August this might prove to be quite complicated. You could try to arrange this through the Kibbutz office in Tel Aviv or through a private office. You will usually need to attend an interview and have the following documents:

1. a valid passport
2. medical certificate saying that you are in good health and able to do physical work
3. two letters of recommendation
4. a return ticket or proof that you have enough money to buy one.

Useful addresses
You could apply for Kibbutz voluntary work through the following:

The Takam (United Kibbutz Movement) Volunteers Department,

18 Frischman Street, Tel Aviv. Tel: 03 5246154 (ask for Reuben Freedman). Office hours: Sunday–Thursday 0800–1400; closed Friday and Saturday.

Ha'kibbutz Ha'dati (The Religious Kibbutzim Movement), 7 Dobnov Street, Tel Aviv. Tel: 03 6957231 (ask for Ilana Lerman). Office hours: Wednesday 0800–1300; other days by appointment. Remember that this movement takes only Jewish volunteers.

WORKING IN A MOSHAV

What is a Moshav?

A Moshav (*pl.* Moshavim) is a settlement where members own land and property and work within a co-operative framework for their own profit. On each Moshav there is a centre where you can find a shop or a mini-market, post office, clinic and sporting facilities; some Moshavim also have a swimming pool.

What is voluntary work in a Moshav?

Moshav volunteers work for a single family in all sorts of work mainly agricultural. Your working hours vary according to demand but basically you will have to work eight hours a day, six days a week.

What will you get in return?

You will get free, usually, self-contained accommodation which you share with two or three other volunteers. Working in a Moshav is not entirely voluntary and you are paid about £200 per month plus overtime if available.

Do you fit the bill?

You have to be aged between 20 and 35, physically and mentally fit and willing to work hard (sometimes overtime) in hard conditions. You should be able to commit yourself for at least eight weeks and willing to live in shared accommodation with other volunteers.

Booking procedure

You could arrange voluntary work in a Moshav from the UK through Project 67. Ask for an application form and further particulars, send the completed application and follow instructions.

How much will it cost?
Project 67's price for fixed return of maximum six months 1996/7 was between £239 and £289; an open return ticket maximum twelve months was between £279 and £299. This did not include £10 airport tax. Travel insurance, which is compulsory, for up to eight weeks was £45, up to three months £60, up to six months £85 and each additional month £22. Included in the price is return flight London–Tel Aviv–London; first placement on a Moshav; initial registration fees; first night in a Tel Aviv hostel; service of the Tel Aviv office.

Useful addresses
UK office: Project 67, 10 Hatton Garden, London EC1N 8AH. Tel: (0171) 831 7626. Fax: (0171) 404 5588.
Israel office: Project 67, 94 Ben Yehuda Street, Tel Aviv. Tel: 03 5230140.

Applying in Israel
Although it is better to apply before you leave home, you can also do so while in Israel, mainly through The Workers Moshavim Movement Volunteer Department which is the official office for recruiting volunteers. It is run by Liora Fein-Hiller. You will have to attend an interview and it might take up to two weeks to place you in a Moshav. You can work for three months and it may be possible to extend your stay for another three months. The registration fee of about £20 will be refunded by the Moshav where you work. Insurance is compulsory.

Useful addresses
The Workers Moshavim Movement Volunteer Department, 19 Leonardo de Vinci Street, Tel Aviv. Tel: 03 6958473 (ask for Liora). Fax: 5241604.
Meira's Volunteers for Moshav, 73 Ben Yehuda Street, Tel Aviv 63435. Tel: 03 5243811.

QUESTIONS AND ANSWERS – KIBBUTZ AND MOSHAV

Are there any age limits?
Yes. 18–32 for a Kibbutz, 20–35 for a Moshav.

Do I need a working visa?
Yes you do. The Kibbutz or Moshav will arrange it for you. You should bring two passport-size photos and be prepared to pay

around £12.50. You can only get a working visa if you have not been a volunteer in Israel within the last year.

Do I need a passport or visa?
UK citizens need a full British passport but no visa. If you hold a second passport, you should contact the Israeli Embassy.

Can I choose the type of work I do in the Kibbutz or Moshav?
No. It depends on what work is available at the time. But you can always ask (don't forget you are now in Israel!) to do certain work and those in charge might take your request into consideration.

What is the minimum stay?
Usually it is eight weeks for both Kibbutz and Moshav volunteers.

When can I go?
Throughout the year. The months of June–September are the busiest ones.

How long does it take to arrange?
Usually between three and five weeks but urgent applications may get priority.

Can I extend my stay?
Yes. If you are already in the Kibbutz or the Moshav they can arrange it for you. Their decision whether to extend your stay will be based on their requirements and your attitude to work and community life in general.

Are there any health requirements?
You must be in good physical and mental health.

Do I need an HIV test?
No, but the Kibbutz reserve the right to request you to take an HIV test.

What about money?
Volunteers receive a small allowance while working in the Kibbutz. Moshav volunteers are paid about £200 per month plus overtime if they are asked to work overtime.

Is insurance necessary?

Insurance which covers both the Kibbutz area and outside it is compulsory. The companies which deal with voluntary work in Israel usually demand that volunteers take out their own policies.

WORKING IN ARCHAEOLOGY

The strange thing about working voluntarily in archaeology is that not only is the work very hard but volunteers have to pay for their flight, insurance, accommodation and often for participating in the work.

What does voluntary work in archaeology involve?
Digging, shovelling, cleaning and hauling pottery and other items. The work is hard and often tedious and starts early in the morning before the heat of the day. Often there are lectures in history, archaeology and geography as well as short trips. You are usually asked to pay a daily charge for food and accommodation although occasionally accommodation is free of charge.

Do you fit the bill?
• Usually (though not always) you should be over 18.
• You should be physically fit and able to work long hours in hot weather conditions.
• You should be able to commit yourself for a minimum of one week and pay a daily charge for food and accommodation.
• You should be highly motivated.

Booking procedure
You should apply in writing indicating the period and vicinity you are interested in (if you know) and the times and dates which suit you. If you are a student of archaeology or an experienced digger, you should mention it in your letter as this may lead to some concessions and more interest in your offer.

Useful addresses
For more details contact the following:

Department of Classical Studies, Prof M. Gichon, Division of Archaeology, Ramat Aviv, 69978, Tel Aviv. Tel: 03 6408111/ 6409111.

Israel Antiquities Authority, PO Box 586, Rockefeller Museum,

Jerusalem 91004. Tel: 6282251.

Jewish National Fund, Eli Shenhav, 11 Zvi Shapira Street, Tel Aviv 64538. Tel: 02 2561129.

Project 67, 10 Hatton Garden, London EC1N 8AH. Tel: (0171) 831 7626. Fax: (0171) 404 5588. This London office organises digs for volunteers at various sites in co-operation with the Israeli Antiquities authority. The cost is from £350 which covers return flight, full board and insurance.

OTHER VOLUNTARY JOBS

Friends of Israel Educational Trust
The organisation offers twelve scholarships per year to enable volunteers to participate in Kibbutz work and do some teaching in a developing town. The scholarships cover travel, board and living. There is no pay and the work involves between five and six hours of teaching per day, six days a week between February and August. You need to enclose a stamped addressed envelope or an international reply coupon by 1 July for the following year. *Address*: 25 Lyndale Ave, London NW2 2QB. Tel: (0171) 435 6803. Fax: (0171) 749 0291.

Israel Youth Hostel Association
If you wish to work as a volunteer in a youth hostel in Israel then here is a good opportunity. Board and accommodation is provided free of charge and some pocket money is also paid in return for a six-hour working day. You should write directly to the youth hostel where you wish to work. A list of youth hostels can be obtained from the following *address*: PO Box 1075, 3 Dorot Rishonim, Jerusalem. Tel: 02 6252706.

CASE STUDIES

John works hard and enjoys his leisure time
John arranged everything before leaving England through the Kibbutz Representatives in London. He asked to be sent to a young Kibbutz, preferably in the Negev. This was arranged and John was sent to Kibbutz Retamim. He was offered the chance to go with a group but preferred to go on his own because he wanted to be in Israel earlier.

John now shares his room with two other volunteers and he works in the *Falcha* (agriculture) with other Kibbutzniks. To avoid the heat of the day they wake up at four in the morning and work until eleven. John then joins the other Kibbutzniks and they all have lunch which is followed by a break. At around four in the afternoon they go to work again (for two hours).

John spends his evenings with friends. They often go to Be'er Sheva (which is only 35 minutes away) and have some fun.

Jill is now working in archeaological excavations
Knowing that the work is hard and often tedious Jill did not plan to work in archaeology. But because Jill can only move to her new rented flat in two weeks time she decided to spend the short period doing some voluntary work. She rang the Israel Antiquities Authority and, luckily for her, they had some vacanices. Jill is now digging, shovelling and hauling pottery fragments and surprisingly enough finds this work quite exciting.

Clair is back in Jerusalem and looking for some new adventures and income
Clair is thinking of working in a Moshav, and although she does not yet know when or where, she has started to gather information. She rang The Workers Moshavim Movement Volunteer Department in Tel Aviv and they promised to send her some information.

DISCUSSION POINTS

1. You are considering voluntary work in Israel. Draw up a list of pros and cons to see if you fit the bill.

2. Look at the Questions and Answers section of this chapter and decide whether you would prefer to work on a Kibbutz or a Moshav.

3. Draw up a list of any other voluntary jobs which might suit you and try to find out more about them before leaving for Israel.

7
Other Job Opportunities

Israel has a relatively lenient immigration policy, you will find several opportunities for work especially in child care, the tourist industry and even teaching English as a foreign language.

WORKING AS AN AU PAIR, NANNY OR MOTHER'S HELP

Visa, work permit and insurance

The Israeli authorities are not very enthusiastic about giving work permits to foreigners wishing to work in child care. In practice, however, there are many foreigners who are employed in this way, especially in the cities and the more prosperous suburbs such as Herzeliyya and Ramat Ha'sharon.

Even if you have a pre-arranged family placement, it is advisable not to ask for the work permit when you enter Israel. Leave it for the family with whom you work, or the agency which places you, to arrange. They can succeed where you might fail.

You will also need comprehensive insurance. Remember that in Israel you cannot just pop into a hospital without paying – and medical care is expensive. Letters of recommendation, preferably from people for whom you worked in the past as an au pair, are very important. A growing number of families and agencies are now asking to see your HIV test.

Your duties and what you get

You should expect to work hard: between eight and nine hours a day, six days a week. You may have to take and bring back the children from school, babysit, and do some housework, cleaning and even cooking simple meals. You will usually be paid monthly and a return fare may be paid after completing one year's contract. You will also be entitled to a certain amount of annual leave.

Hunting for a job

There are three ways of finding a child care position in Israel:

1. advertisements
2. word of mouth
3. agencies.

Looking at the ads

The best plan is to look for a job while still in Britain. Look at the ads in the *Jewish Chronicle*, which is published every Friday and can be found in many shops in North London (Golders Green, Hendon) and in big bookshops situated close to Jewish communities. Also look in *The Lady* where openings in Israel are often advertised.

If in Israel, look in the local papers and at the ads of the English daily *The Jerusalem Post*. Look also for advertisements on the noticeboards in Tel Aviv hostels, on trees, and especially in your local shop and supermarket. You could also place your own ads in a local or national newspaper. To do so, ring the switchboard of the newspaper in which you wish to place your ad and ask for specific information (style, price).

Useful address
The Jerusalem Post, Romema, Jerusalem 91000. Tel: 02 5315666.

Doing it the Israeli way

A common Israeli method of looking for a job, including au pairing, is word of mouth. Hang around and look around; ask in your local shop; go to a nursery and ask if they know of any opening; ask your neighbours. This method which combines word of mouth and informal, straightforward inquiry is acceptable in Israel.

Using an agency

This is perhaps the easiest way to find a job as an au pair in Israel, but it does have its drawbacks. The great advantage of an agency is that it has access, connections and experience and can not only place you but also provide important advice regarding visa, work permit, cheap flights and so on. The main disadvantage is that you are less in control. You are *placed* rather than *choosing* the family which you feel matches you, although having said that, any contract you sign is with the family and not with the agency.

There are agencies in Britain and Israel which place girls to work as au pairs. Agencies in Britain usually charge you for their service; this is not usually the case in Israel. If you do decide to use an agency to find an au pairing job in Israel, all you have to do is phone them or send a letter (preferably with self-addressed envelope) stating when you want to go and to where and asking for more particulars.

Useful addresses
In Israel
Star Au Pair International, 16 Michal Street, Tel Aviv 63261. Tel: 03 6291748, 03 6201195, 052 452002 (David Star). You must be at least 21, having recommendations and clear HIV test. A driving licence is an advantage. Salary negotiable.

Au Pair International, 2 Desler Street, B'nei B'rak 51507. Tel: 03 6190423. This agency can place you as a nanny, mother's help or housekeeper. Usually the contract is for one year with board and accommodation provided. You need to be between 19–45 and have full health insurance.

'Babayit' nannies and foreign workers, 26 Rambam Street, Tel Aviv. Tel: 03 5289990. 62/5 Bialik Street, Ramat Gan. Tel: 03 6720697. 17 Hovevai Zion Street, Petach Tiqva. Tel: 03 9340275.

Danel, 98 Dizingoff Street, Tel Aviv. Tel: 03 5222266.

In the UK
Anglia Au Pair and Domestic Agency, 15 Eastern Avenue, Southend-on-Sea, Essex SS2 5QX. Tel: (01702) 613888 (or 471648).

Basil Recruitment Bureau, 13 Knightsbridge Green, London SW1X 7QL. Tel: (0171) 581 4393.

Checklist
Before taking any job as an au pair, try to find out more about the following points:

• What is the wage and when and how are you paid?

• Do you have to pay for your food and accommodation?

- How many hours does the work entail?

- Are you expected to do cleaning, cooking and babysitting, and will you be paid extra money for these jobs?

- Are you entitled to holidays?

- What happens if you are ill?

- Are you allowed to bring friends to your room and are they allowed to stay overnight?

- Is there a policy on smoking?

- Are you entitled to free return fare and how long do you need to work before having this right?

WORKING IN THE TOURIST INDUSTRY

Tourism is an important market in Israel and offers some very good opportunities for work. The places where you are most likely to find a job are Eilat, Jerusalem and Tel Aviv.

Eilat is Israel's holiday resort and during the main season, which is between October and March, you could look for a job in a hotel or restaurant. Just show up, ask to speak to the manager, introduce yourself and ask if there is any job available at the moment. You need to remember, though, that in Eilat the competition is fierce and wages are relatively low.

If you are qualified as a diver you could look for a job as an instructor in one of the diving centres, while women can look for jobs as hostesses in one of these places.

Jerusalem also offers opportunities for the job-seeker. Try one of the very many hotels. You can also look for a job in the eastern part of the city, although wages there are often lower than in the western part.

In **Tel Aviv** most of the hotels are situated along the beach. Again the best way to find a job is by word of mouth and showing up at the hotels asking if there are any openings. If you have a permanent address you can also send a letter asking for a job. You could also try to find a job in a restaurant. Try Dizingoff Street, Sheinkin Street and the Marina.

TEACHING ENGLISH AS A FOREIGN LANGUAGE

This could be for you (at least at the beginning) a complementary job. If you manage to get one pupil you could ask him or her to spread the word so you can get more pupils. Try to advertise in your local paper, put notes on boards in Tel Aviv, Jerusalem, Bar Illan or Be'er Sheva Universities, as well as in your local shop and the supermarket. Do not put a note on one of the trees in Dizingoff Street; this was a method used in the past until the council began sending its people to locate those hanging these ads and punish them. You should also look at the noticeboards in tourists' hostels.

CASE STUDIES

Jill is now working in a hotel in Tel Aviv

After finding a lovely flat in south Tel Aviv and thus acquiring a permanent address, she sent some letters to five hotels in Tel Aviv. She also showed up, asked to talk to the manager, introduced herself and asked for a job. She always took with her recommendations and her Curriculum Vitae which showed that she has some experience in hotel management. The other day Jill received a letter from one of the most respectable hotels in Tel Aviv offering her a job as a receptionist. Jill gladly accepted the offer.

John fell in love with the Kibbutz and they fell in love with him

John is working in farming and because he is such a valuable worker, the Kibbutz managed to extend his visa. John plans to stay for another three months and then buy a second hand car and travel in Israel, the Sinai and Jordan.

Clair is now working as a waitress

She has not yet abandoned the idea of spending some time in a Moshav, but she cannot afford it now, because to do so she needs to leave Jerusalem for at least eight weeks. To earn some money she went to Ben Yehuda Street in Jerusalem where there are many tourist restaurants. Her Hebrew is so good now that she could even ask the manager in Hebrew: 'Atem Tzrichim Meltzarit?' meaning, 'Do you need a waitress?' She was offered a part-time job as a waitress.

DISCUSSION POINTS

1. You wish to work as an au pair in Israel. Try to weigh the pros and cons of using an agency to find a job, or doing it yourself. Decide your course of action.

2. You wish to work in the tourist industry. Try to decide between the following places, taking into account your personal requirements and the weather conditions: Eilat, Tel Aviv, Jerusalem.

3. Write a letter in Hebrew (maybe with the help of an Israeli friend) to five hotel managers. Introduce yourself and ask if there are any openings. Type your letter and attach your Curriculum Vitae.

8
Living in Israel

SHOPPING IN ISRAEL

Understanding VAT

Value Added Tax (17 per cent in 1996) is levied on all goods and services and is included in the quoted price.

As a newcomer you are exempt from VAT on the following services if paid for in foreign currency: accommodation (hotels, youth hostels, field schools and camping); organised tours; tourist car hire with driver guide; car rental; flights and tours operated by inland aviation companies; meals provided by tour operators during organised tours; meals eaten in hotel restaurants by guests.

If you purchase goods with foreign currency exceeding $50 in value at shops recommended by the Ministry of Tourism, you are entitled to a discount of at least 5 per cent off the purchase price at the shop and a VAT refund at the port of departure. You should remember, however, to obtain a receipt from the shop, indicating the amount of VAT paid in US dollars (rounded to the nearest dollar) less commission.

Remember also that Eilat is a tax-free zone which means that all items are exempt from VAT and purchase tax. Items you might see in chain stores in Tel Aviv or Jerusalem will be cheaper in Eilat.

There are also reductions on specific items and cashback on such purchases can be claimed from: The Department of Customs, 32 Agron Street, Jerusalem 944190.

Shopping at markets

If you want to buy cheap fruit and vegetables you should go to the markets at Tel Aviv (*Shuk Ha'Carmel*) or Jerusalem (*Shuk Machané Yehuda*). Small towns also have markets for fruit and vegetables. While the prices in the *Shuk* are usually lower than in the supermarket, you must watch out that you pay no more than you should. Prices in these markets drop dramatically on Friday afternoons when the sellers try to get rid of their goods before the Shabath.

The Bedouin Market in Be'er Sheva is another place to go, have fun and buy at cheap prices. The market is held on Thursdays only opening at daybreak and running until early afternoon. The best time to get there is at 0600 in the summer and 0700 in the winter. The range of goods is enormous and covers woven camel bags, earrings, bracelets, amulets and nose rings, copper ware, coin headbands, beaded bags and embroidered dresses. Getting a bargain in this market means haggling. A rule of thumb is that you should end up paying 20 per cent to 30 per cent less than the original asking price.

Shopping at the Jerusalem Mall
If you are addicted to mall shopping, the Jerusalem Mall can satisfy most of your needs. It has nearly 200 shops and food outlets, and lays claim to the distinction of being the largest shopping mall in the Middle East. The best advice from locals is: never buy gold, silver or gems in the Jerusalem Mall because you will almost always over-pay.

Opening hours
Things have changed quite dramatically in the last few years. While all shops used to close between 1300 and 1600 nowadays most stores are open continuously Sundays to Thursdays between 0830–0900 and 1900, and Fridays until about 1400. Many of the supermarkets are open until after 2100 on Thursdays; some remain open much later.

• Do remember that on Friday afternoons (starting from about 1400), Saturdays and Jewish holidays, all shopping enterprises are closed.

Antiques
Antiques are defined in Israel law as man-made objects fashioned before 1700 CE. Such items may not be taken out of Israel (whether personally or by mail) without the written approval of the Director of Antiquities Authority. A 10 per cent export fee is levied on the purchase price.

For more details contact: The Antiquities Authority, Rockefeller Museum, PO Box 586, Jerusalem 91004. Tel: 02 6282251.

Newspapers
There are more than twenty daily newspapers in Israel many of which are in Hebrew. You can find European newspapers, especially in Jerusalem and Tel Aviv in the bookshops of *Stematzki*. British newspapers appear on the shelf one day later.

BUYING AND USING A CAR

Cars are expensive to buy and maintain in Israel. If you want to buy a new car you should contact an agent who specialises in importing the car you wish to buy; you can find the relevant address in the *Yellow Pages* under 'Cars' (there is a section written in English). Also look at the advertisements in your local or national paper for deals.

If you want to buy a second-hand used car the choice is vast. The first things you have to ask yourself is what car would be best for you.

What car would be best?

The following questions might help you identify the sort of car that best suit you:

1. *Size and type of car* – A family car with space for luggage or shopping? A hatchback, estate or a saloon?

2. *Maintenance and running costs* – Do you want to carry out services yourself? If not, can you afford to run a car with high service costs?

3. *Personal preferences* – Do you prefer automatic transmission and/or power steering? Do you need lots of head-or leg-room? Do you need luxuries like a sunroof or electric windows, or would you be happy with a low-spec model?

If you have managed to answer these questions then you do know what you want to buy and the only thing for you now is to find where to buy.

Where to buy

You can buy either from a dealer or from a private seller. Most Israelis buy from private sellers.

Buying from a dealer

Buying from a dealer is convenient – there are lots of cars to look at and you do not have to spend a lot of time looking for the one you want. In addition, most dealers are able to check that a used car does not have any outstanding problems. The drawback, though, is that buying from a dealer means a more expensive price because the dealers has to cover his overheads and make a profit.

If you do intend to use a dealer, look in the *Yellow Pages*, or at ads in the national papers. Many cars held by dealers are ex-company and ex-rental cars; these are a bit cheaper to buy and sell. You have to check the documents to see if the car is ex-rental or ex-company and pay accordingly (about 10 per cent cheaper than a car bought from a private seller).

Buying from a private seller
Cars sold privately are usually cheaper than those sold by dealers. To find a used car all you have to do is look in the local and national papers, *Ma'ariv*, *Yediot Ahronot*, *Ha'aretz* and *The Jerusalem Post*. The best plan is to look in the weekend papers and also on Tuesdays. Israelis wishing to buy used cars would usually get the papers on Thursday night or early Friday morning (remember in Israel the weekend starts on Friday and weekend papers are printed on Thursday night) in order to be the first to ring. It is also very useful to buy one of the monthly car magazines which publish up-to-date prices of used cars.

When you find the car which seems to match your requirements, phone and ask for more details.

The telephone conversation
Do not hesitate to ask if the seller speaks English; most Israelis do. Your first question should be

● 'Is the car still for sale?' (Ha-im Ha-me-chonit a-daiin li-me-chi-ra?)

followed by questions about:

● the model (eizé-model?)

● engine size (ne-fach ma-noaa?)

● year (ei-zé sha-na Ha-me-chonit?)

● kilometres (ma Ha-kilometrazh?)

● colour (Tz-eva?)

● accident damage (Ha-im Ha-me-cho-nit Achrei te-una?)

● when the Test (MOT equivalent) expires (ka-ma ze-man Ha-test?)

• how many previous owners it has had (Ka-ma be-alim ko-dmim?)

• why the car is for sale? (La-ma Ha'me-cho-nit le-mechi-ra?)

Put your questions politely but don't accept evasive answers like: 'It is my grandma's car, but she is not here now – she died.' Do not make an appointment to view a car unless the seller gives you satisfactory answers.

There are traders who present themselves as private sellers. You can easily spot them. A genuine private seller will answer your questions easily, but the dodgy trader with several cars to sell will have trouble identifying which car you are referring to.

Arranging a visit

Find out as much as possible on the phone, as this may save a wasted visit (probably early on Friday morning) to view an unsuitable car. If the car sounds right, ask for the seller's name and address and arrange a visit.

You want to try and be the first one to view the car; firstly, because if this is a good car then you do not want anyone else to buy it; secondly, because if you do decide to take the car and wish to check it out at a garage, then you must start very early in the morning (most cars are bought on Friday, and garages close early because of the Shabath). In short, try to arrange an early visit to view the car and when you arrive, ignore the other people who have also come to view the car.

Checking out the car

If you are not confident of your ability to check a used car and negotiate a deal, ask someone with more knowledge, preferably an Israeli, to accompany you. Two pairs of eyes are better than one, and knowledge of the language can only help. Always view in daylight, and never inspect a car under artificial light.

You should always take the car for an independent inspection. Brush aside the seller's suggestion that you go to his garage (he will say: 'I know the garage . . . it will be much quicker') and ask to go to an **MMM** or **Dinamometre** garage. If the seller won't agree to an inspection, assume that there is a problem with the car.

Remember that you will have to pay for the check-up even if you decide as a result not to buy the car. From my own experience, however, it is always worth spending some money before buying a used car.

If the car fails to impress you, look elsewhere. Don't hesitate to ask for a reduction in price if you feel small defects need attention. The seller may be prepared to drop the price a little. Having struck a deal, get the seller to confirm the details in writing. The safest way to pay is by cheque, as a seller wanting cash may be a shady dealer. The next stage is to transfer the car into your name. You will do that together with the seller in a post office or a bank. Once the car is in your name, the next stage is to insure it. Shop around for the best deal. Look in the *Yellow Pages* under 'car insurance'.

Maintaining your car

This is an expensive business. Once a year you have to take your car for an Israeli Test (equivalent to the British MOT). Try to find a good local garage after shopping around and asking friends. You can also look in the *Yellow Pages*.

Road assistance is not very common in Israel. One company which does provide the service is Hagorer, 66 Derech Petach, Tikva, Tel Aviv. Tel: 03 6871919.

Driving your car

It is most important that before setting off you make every effort to familiarise yourself with Israeli local laws and customs of driving. Here are some tips:

- **In Israel you drive on the RIGHT.** You may have driven on the right before, but this could be your first time with a left-hand drive model. You may find it difficult judging the distance on your right-hand side. Ask a passenger to help with this problem. Changing gear with the 'wrong' hand can feel awkward too, so an automatic is a good option. If it is your first experience with an automatic, remember to use your right foot for *both* brake and accelerator. In addition, automatics creep forward unless you keep your foot on the brake. Remember that you drive on the *right* and overtake on the *left*.

- **Speed limit.** The speed limit in built-up areas is 50 km/31 miles an hour. Outside built-up areas it is 80 km/50 miles an hour, or 90 km/56 miles an hour where so marked.

- **Safety belts.** Safety belts must be worn by you and your passengers in both the front and the rear seats.

• **Flashing the headlights signals an intention to go, *not* to give way.**
  Do remember that the Israelis use their headlights to signal when
  they are claiming the right of way. Flashing the headlights is *not*
  an invitation to pass. Rather it means 'Move over, I am coming
  through and you had better stop...otherwise...' A flash of lights
  from an oncoming driver may also be a friendly warning to you of
  nearby speed traps.

• **Pedestrians.** It is almost a rule of thumb that Israelis ignore the
  rights of pedestrians. This is especially true at zebra crossings which
  is one of the most dangerous places to cross a busy street in Israel. If
  you do decide to stop at a zebra crossing to allow pedestrians to
  cross (which is a very sensible thing to do) make sure that the car
  behind you is not too close – even though it is the responsibility of
  that driver to allow enough space for stopping safely.

• **Parking.** Be sure you understand parking restrictions, especially
  in the big cities. Towing away and clamping is increasingly being
  used, especially in Tel Aviv. You can buy parking cards in kiosks
  or post offices. Scratch off the date and time of arrival on the
  parking card and display it behind the windscreen. You can park
  where the kerb is painted blue-white.

What to do if you have an accident

If you are involved in an accident, the most important thing is to
keep calm and ignore the fact that the other party is probably going
to lose their temper, even if [s]he is to be blamed for the accident.
Then take the following actions:

• Alert other traffic by setting a warning triangle and switching on
  your car's hazard lights.

• If anyone has been injured, arrange for someone to call an
  ambulance and the police.

• Record all particulars of the accident including: names and
  addresses of witnesses, damage to the vehicles involved, name
  and address of the other driver, name and address of the other
  party's insurance company and number of the insurance
  certificate, registration number of the other vehicle, date, time
  and location of the accident, speed of the vehicles involved,

details of the road and the weather at the time of the accident. Draw a sketch of the accident and if you have a camera take a picture of the scene. Remember not to make any admission of responsibility for the accident and never sign *any* document, let alone one which is in Hebrew.

GOING OUT

Do not look for night life in Jerusalem. Tel Aviv is the Israeli centre for night life with numerous discos, bars, jazz clubs and so on. Things are on the move in Tel Aviv; in the past the centre of night life was in the western part of town but now it is concentrated more to the south. Cinema is very popular in Israel and there are local and international films with subtitles in Hebrew. You can buy tickets to all events through agencies or at the box office on the night of the show.

Useful addresses (Tel Aviv unless otherwise mentioned.)
Night clubs
Barekod, 14 Ha'arbat. Tel: 03 5612988. All types of music, not including techno and acid, ages 25 +.
Elizabeth, Jaffa Port. Tel 03 814752. All types of music, ages 22 +.
Former Allenby Cinema, 54 Allenby Street. Afternoon party for ages 25 +. Tel: 03 5173788.
Camelot, 16 Shalmon Aleichem Street. Tel: 03 5285222. High class blues jazz club, live music every night.
Lemon, 16 Shalmon Aleichem Street. Tel: 03 6813313.
Santa Fe, 61 Ha'yarkon Street. Tel: 03 5160222. Ages 25 +.
Zeman Amiti, 8 Eilat Street. Tel: 03 6837788, 6810231.

Night clubs – ethnic
Caesar, 193 Dizengoff Street. Tel: 03 5245106. Greek, ages 30 +.
Fresco, 11 Rabmbam Street. Tel: 03 5163764. Oriental club, Israeli songs, ages 30 +.
Jamaica, 58 Ha'masger Street. Tel: 03 5621691. Israeli songs, Reggae, ages 18 +.
Soweto, 6 Friesman Street. Tel: 03 5240825. Reggae and black music, ages change.

Games – bowling
American Bowling Centre, Ramat Gan Stadium (Gate 2). Tel: 03 5700834.

Petach Tikva Bowling, 7 Basel Street, Petach Tikva. Tel: 03 9242615.
Rehovot Bowling, 33 Mosher Yatumm, Rehovot. Tel: 08 9460397.
Superbowl, 19 Saharov Street, Rishon le Zion. Tel: 03 9624958.
Bowling Centre, Kiriat Arie, Petach Tikva. Tel: 03 9242615.

Bridge
Association for Furthering Bridge, American House, 35 Shaul
    Ha'melech. Tel: 03 6956171.
Beit Bridge, 14 Carlebach Street. Tel: 03 5621348.
Country Gimmel, 8 Einstein Street, Ramat Aviv Gimmel. Tel: 03
    6417469, 6417470.
Kfar Ha'maccabia, Kfar Ha'maccabia, Ramat Gan. Tel: 03
    6715715.
Naamat Givataim, 20 Mishmar Ha'yarden, Givatayim. Tel: 03
    5719754.
Ramat Gan Club, 2 Mirkin Corner, Ha'roe, Ramat Gan. Tel: 03
    6722359.
Rowal Cafe, 111 Dizengoff Street. Tel: 03 524 3410.
Ulpan Ha'bridge, 71 Iben Grirol Street. Tel: 03 5279147.

Kwaizer
This is a group laser war game, played in a hall and including
padding and rifles. Length of game about half an hour. *Address*: 10
Ben Gurion Street, near Canyon Ayalon, Ramat Gan. Tel: 03
7523325.

Chess
Bikurei Ha'itim, 6 Haftman Street. Tel: 03 6919510, 6919457.
Moetzet Po'alai Givataim, 18 Weitzmann Street, Givataim. Tel: 03
    318698.

Scrabble
Wizo House, 132 Ha'nassi Street, Herzelliya Pituach. Tel: 09
    576634, 557302.

Video games
Dizengoff Centre 'A', just outside the centre in Dizengoff Street.
Dizengoff Centre 'B', Galaxy, inside the centre near King George
    Street.
Opera Tower, Opera Tower, 1 Allenby Street, ground floor.

SPORT

Diving

The coasts of the Red Sea off Eilat offer magnificent diving grounds throughout the year. Various diving schools offer courses for beginners and for more experienced divers. Snorkelling and scuba diving equipment can be hired on the spot. The diving season on the Mediterranean coast of Israel is from March to May with Rosh Ha'niqra in northern Israel offering some most interesting attractions.

Useful addresses
Andromeda Diving Centre, Jaffa Harbour, Tel Aviv. Tel: 03 6827572.
Snapir Diving Centre, Jaffa Harbour, Tel Aviv. Tel: 03 6050366.
Shiqmona Diving Club, Kishon Harbour, Haifa. Tel: 04 8323911.
Caesarea Diving Club, Roman Harbour. Tel: 06 361441.
Aqua Sport Red Sea Diving Centre, Coral Beach, Eilat. Tel: 07 334404.
Red Sea Sport, King Solomon Quay, Eilat. Tel: 07 6376569.
Gal Mor Caesarea, The Old Town. Tel: 06 361787.

Golf

There is a fine 18-hole golf course at Caesarea, near the site of ancient Caesarea. You could be admitted as a temporary member. For more information, Tel: 06 361172.

Mini-golf

Golfitek, Rokach Boulevard, Ramat Aviv, Tel Aviv. Tel: 03 6990229.
Golfitek, end of Ben Gurion, between Ramat Ha'sharon and Herzliyya. Tel: 09 554402.
Mini Golf, National (Leumi) Park, near the Safara, Ramat Gan. Tel: 03 6314126.

Riding

There is a growing number of riding schools in Israel. Some offer guided treks; other just hire out horses and teach you how to ride. Upper Galilee offers good riding country.

Useful addresses
Havat Amir, Atarot Jerusalem. Tel: 02 5824769.
King David's Riding Stables, Neve Illan. Tel: 02 5340535.

Ha'shmura, Beit Hanan. Tel: 03 9560011.
Havat Liron, Moshav Rishpon. Tel: 09 507235.
Havat Mechora, Hof Ha'Carmel. Tel: 04 9842735.

Tennis

In Ramat Ha'sharon, near Tel Aviv, you can find plenty of tennis courts. Several hotels feature tennis courts as well.

Useful addresses
Ramat Ha'sharon (24 courts). Tel: 03 6456666.
Jerusalem (19 courts). Tel: 02 6791866.
Tel Aviv (17 courts). Tel: 03 6491337.
Ashkelon (17 courts). Tel: 07 672228.
Haifa (24 courts). Tel: 04 8522721.
Arad (7 courts). Tel: 07 9956877.
Qiryat Shemona (8 courts). Tel: 06 949034.
Tiberias (6 courts). Tel: 06 73154.

Surfing

You can practise surfing along Israel's Mediterranean coast, especially near the town of Nahariya where the world championship was held in 1980. You can also try surfing in Eilat and on the Sea of Galilee.

Skiing

Israel's winter sports area is in the north of the country, on Mount Hermon, which rises to 8,500 ft on the Israeli side. The season is from December until mid-April. In the nearby Moshav, Neve Ativ, you can hire the necessary equipment and take a ski course.

STAYING ON THE HEALTHY SIDE

Medical aid

Medical care is very good throughout Israel. There is, however, no social security agreement with Britain and medical treatment must be paid for on the spot; so make sure that when you go to Israel you are insured. If you stay for a longer period check the possibility of joining the country's health insurance; for example the **Histadrut** or **Macabi**.

If you need emergency treatment, look in the daily press which carries listings of duty rosters for emergency hospitals, dental clinics and pharmacies which are open at night, weekends and holidays.

Emergency numbers
- Dial 101 in most major urban areas for emergency or first aid assistance provided by *Magen David Adom* (the Red Star of David – Israel's equivalent to the Red Cross).

- For intensive care ambulance service dial 03 5460111 (Tel Aviv); 02 561303 (Jerusalem); 04 8672222 (Haifa).

- For *Shaal*, a private intensive care service for heart patients serving the Greater Tel Aviv, Haifa and Jerusalem metropolitan areas, dial 03 5625555.

Other medical services include:

- Eran (mental health hotline)   1201
- Rape Crisis Centre   04 8530533
- Open Door (sex advice for youth)   03 5101411
- Hand in Hand (child hotline)   03 5226027
- Alcoholics Anonymous   03 5225255
- Narcotics Anonymous   03 5758869

Life for the disabled
Facilities for disabled people have much improved in Israel in the last few years. Many places including Ben Gurion International Airport, provide ramps, specially equipped lavatories, telephones and other conveniences for the handicapped. **Milbat**, The Advisory Centre for the Disabled at Sheeba Medical Centre in Tel Aviv, can help you with more information. **Yad Sarah**, Israel's largest voluntary organisation, offers free loan of medical and rehabilitative equipment; a certain donation is required in return.

Useful addresses
The Royal Association for Disability and Rehabilitation (RADAR), 25 Mortimer Street, London W1N 8AB. Tel: (0171) 637 5400.
The Spinal Injuries Association, 76 St James's Lane, London N10 3DF. Tel: (0181) 444 2122.
Mobility International, 62 Union Street, London SE1. Tel: (0171) 403 5688.
Milbat, The Advisory Centre for the Disabled, Sheeba Medical Centre, Tel Aviv. Tel: 03 5303739.
Yad Sarah, 43 Ha'neviim Street, Jerusalem 95141. Tel: 02 244242. Fax: 02 244493.

CASE STUDIES

John buys a second-hand car

He looked first in his local papers but failed to find anything, so early on Friday morning he looked at the ads in the *Ma'ariv* newspaper and after short inquiry went to view a car on offer. He negotiated the price and then together with the seller went to the MMM centre in Ramat Gan, where the car was independently checked. The car was OK, but there were some repairs to be done, the cost of which was deducted from the price. On Sunday John will transfer the car to his name and insure it. He plans to go on a three-day trip on Monday.

Clair visits the Bedouin market in Be'er Sheva.

She went early on Thursday morning and spent the whole day there. Clair bought woven camel-hair bags, beaded bags and embroidered dresses. It took Clair some time to understand that getting a bargain means haggling; after spending a lot of money on the first item she learnt the trick and the rest of the shopping was quite cheap.

Jill works very hard at the hotel

Jill hardly sees her little rented flat, but she spends a lot of time in the many night clubs in Tel Aviv.

DISCUSSION POINTS

1. You wish to buy a second-hand car. Answer the questions on page 86 to decide which car suits you best.

2. Draw up a list of the questions you intend to ask before going to view the car you hope to buy.

3. Prepare a list of the things you will have to do in case of an accident in Israel. Attach a pencil to this list and put it in the glove compartment – just in case...

9
Education

UNDERSTANDING THE ISRAELI EDUCATION SYSTEM

Israel's education system is comprised of one year of pre-nursery (which is state-optional); one year of nursery (free and compulsory); six years of primary and three years of intermediate school; three years of secondary (or high) school and finally higher education studies (see Figure 9). Schooling in Israel is free and attendance is obligatory for children aged between five and seventeen.

CHOOSING A NURSERY

Israel has one of the highest rates of pre-school attendance in the world with nearly 90 per cent of all three-year-olds and 97 per cent of all four-year-olds attending some form of pre-school programme. Many programmes are sponsored by local authorities; some operate within day-care centres; others are privately owned.

The curriculum aims to teach the children fundamental skills, including language and numerical concepts, to foster cognitive and creative capacities and to promote social abilities. The curricula of all pre-schools are guided and supervised by the Ministry of Education and Culture.

Choosing the right place for your child

First you need to obtain names and addresses of nurseries in your locality. Word of mouth is the recommended method. You could also ask in your local shop. Then visit a few nurseries. Telephone to arrange a meeting. Try to ensure that the headteacher is there when you come to visit.

A very important factor in choosing a nursery is the impression given by the headteacher. When you visit try to see if she is involved in the activities. Does she speak with the children? Is there a sense of organisation, purpose and direction? Is the nursery tidy and well

Percentages of total school population by types of school

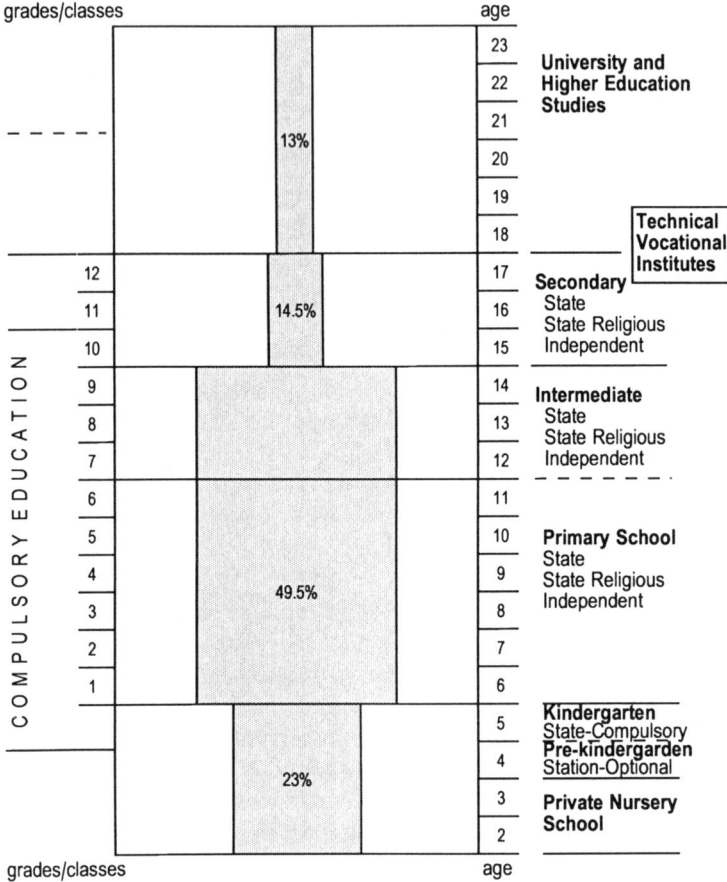

Fig. 9. Israeli school years.

maintained? Above all you want to gain a 'feel' for the nursery and its atmosphere.

Checklist
The following points and questions may help you in your inquiries:

- Organisations to which the nursery belongs
- Ratio of teachers to children
- Qualifications of the staff
- Attitude to religion
- Extra-curricular activities

- Visits arranged away from the nursery
- Timetable and term dates
- Timetable during the day
- Whether the children sleep during the day
- Whether the nursery provides lunch
- Cost.

If you are happy with the atmosphere and satisfied with the approach take the next step and register your child.

CHOOSING A SCHOOL

Two school systems are maintained in Israel: the Jewish system, with instruction in Hebrew, and the Arab/Druze system, with instruction in Arabic. Both systems are financed by and accountable to the Ministry of Education and Culture but enjoy a large measure of internal independence.

The Jewish school system

The Jewish education system consists of state schools, state-religious schools and government-recognised independent religious schools. The state and state-religious schools offer similar academic curricula, with the latter placing special emphasis on Jewish studies, tradition and observance. State schools are co-educational, while in the state-religious school network children may attend either mixed or separate schools. The independent schools, affiliated to various Orthodox Jewish communities, offer more intensive religious instruction and provide separate premises for girls and boys. In recent years, some schools have been established within the education system which reflect specific values, such as liberal Judaism or principles of open education. There are also many independent schools emphasising certain subjects such as art, natural science, and so on. In the mid-1990s nearly 80 per cent of the Jewish school age population attended state schools, some 15 per cent study at state-religious schools, with the rest in independent schools.

The Arab-Druze system

The Arab/Druze education system, with separate schools for Arab and Druze pupils, provides the standard academic and vocational curricula, adapted to emphasise Arab or Druze culture and history. Religious instruction in Islam or Christianity is provided by Arab schools, while in Druze schools such instruction is the prerogative of the community elders. Because of the compulsory Education Law and changes in traditional Arab/Druze attitudes towards formal education, there has been a substantial increase in general school attendance, particularly at the high school level, and in the number of girl pupils, including those remaining through the upper grades. Vocational training in Arab/Druze schools has been expanded, with a variety of subject options geared to practical requirements and the needs of their communities.

Your choices at high school level
At high school level your child can choose one of the following tracks/options:

• Academic track, leading to matriculation exams.

• Technological-vocational track, leading to various technicians' certificates. Three levels exist: graduates of the first level are equipped to continue their studies at institutions of higher education; those at the second level earn a vocational diploma; while those at the third level acquire practical skills.

• Agricultural schools, usually residential, which supplement basic studies with subjects relating to agronomy. Matriculation optional.

• Military preparatory schools, combining general studies with military subjects. Some schools are designed to prepare future career personnel; others to provide skills required by various IDF branches.

• Yeshiva, religious academy for boys, with a curriculum of intensive study of the Bible, Talmud and other Jewish sources, combined with secular studies. The majority are boarding schools.

• Gifted children, who rank in the top 3 per cent of their class and have passed qualifying tests, participate in enrichment programmes, ranging from full-time special schools or extra-curricular courses. Children in these programmes learn to research and handle new material independently.

• Physically, mentally or learning disabled children are placed either in the regular education system or in special settings according to their educational ability and the severity of their handicaps. The aim is to help them function to the best of their abilities and achieve maximum integration into the social and vocational life of the community. Eligibility of handicapped children for special education programmes and facilities, which are free from age 3 to 21, is determined by a committee constituted by law and appointed by the Minister of Education.

Choosing the right school for your child

Usually your child will go to the local (primary or intermediate) school so you will have only a little chance of really choosing a school for him. However, as there are now many new private schools in Israel, it might well be that you decide to send your child to one of them.

Whether you are looking for a primary, intermediate or secondary school for your child the things you have to do are basically the same.

First decide what type of school fits the needs of your child. Try to find out about the school by talking to other parents; this is a most reliable Israeli method of finding out just about everything.

Arranging a visit

However much information may be gained by talking to other people, there is no substitute for a personal visit to the school. Make sure that when you visit the headteacher is present because it is extremely important to judge his or her personality.

It is a good sign if you are instinctively attracted to the school at first sight. But even if it passes this test, and conforms to what you are looking for in terms of location and academic, pastoral and extra-curricular aspects, you will need to satisfy yourself that the school does measure up to what your instincts tell you.

When visiting the school try, as much as you can, to find out what goes on in the school, what is its general ethos and atmosphere. Is there a sense of organisation or a total mess? Is the school tidy and well maintained? Is the pupils' work displayed on the walls? Are there any areas in which the school truly excels? If you are looking for a boarding place, you want to find out how your child will be accommodated. With how many other children will he or she share a room? What activities are provided outside lesson time and at weekends?

Checklist

The following points and questions may help you in your inquiries:

- Overall atmosphere – whether your child will fit in
- Organisation to which the school belongs
- Ratio of teachers to pupils
- Qualifications of the teaching staff
- How often the school communicates with parents through reports, parent/teacher meetings or other visits
- How the school copes with pupils' problems
- Whether progress is accelerated for the academically bright
- How the school copes with pupils who do not work
- Attitude to religion
- Sports offered and standard of facilities
- Extra-curricular activities
- Cultural or other visits arranged away from the school
- How specific talent in music, the arts or sports is encouraged
- The uniform
- Timetable and term dates.

GOING TO POST-SECONDARY SCHOOL EDUCATION

A wide network of post-secondary school educational institutes offer training in nursing, practical engineering, management, computers and other skills. Yeshivas offer a full course of study leading to rabbinical ordination (only for Jews).

Adult education

Education for adults is available in a variety of frameworks. Programmes range from classes providing instruction in basic educational skills and vocational courses to community colleges offering diploma level programmes. The Open University offers courses for credit by correspondence and via radio and television. Look in the *Yellow Pages* for addresses and ask for more information.

Hebrew language instruction

As knowledge of the language is essential to help integrate the many people constantly arriving from all over the world, the Ulpan method was developed. It consists of an intensive course, usually of five months' duration, in which most newcomers acquire adequate proficiency for everyday communication. Not all the courses are open to the public but if you wish to study the language it is always worth trying to get onto one of these courses. (See also Chapter 4.)

Vocational training

The rapid pace of technological development has made vocational and professional training a vital aspect of adult education. Courses at various levels and in-service training are offered to introduce new techniques and knowledge, as well as for occupational retraining geared to meet the changing needs of the economy. Look at the ads for openings.

Enrichment education

Adult education as a leisure activity is becoming more and more popular in Israel. The Ministry of Education and Culture, academic institutions, trade unions, religious institutions and others offer courses, seminars, field trips and the like geared to the requirements of various age and interest groups. Look at the ads for openings.

As already mentioned, many of the above courses are designed for specific populations, but if you are determined to join them and are persistent, the chances are that you might get a place.

GOING TO HIGHER EDUCATION

The higher education system includes universities, institutions granting bachelor degrees only, and courses in regional colleges, as well as other institutes which specialise in such fields as fine arts, music, graphic design, teaching, nursing, advanced technology, agriculture, fashion design and the like. All of these frameworks are accorded full academic and administrative freedom by law and are open to all those who meet their academic requirements.

If you are lacking the necessary qualifications you may attend year-long preparatory programmes offered by the universities; successful completion might enable you to apply for university admission.

Universities

The academic year is between October and July and as a foreign student you should have qualifications equivalent to the Israeli 'Bagrut' (matriculation) certificate for admission. Good knowledge of Hebrew is essential but there are preparatory and orientation courses. Intensive language courses are available. Initiation and orientation programmes are also organised by Departments of Overseas Students in institutions of higher learning. The universities are listed in Figure 10, together with their year of opening and number of students (1995 figures).

University	Year of opening	No. of students
Technion-Israel, Institute of Technology, Haifa	1924	9,000
Haifa University, Haifa	1963	6,000
Hebrew University, Jerusalem	1925	16,000
Bar-Ilan University, Ramat Gan	1955	10,000
Tel Aviv University, Ramat Aviv	1956	16,900
Ben Gurion University of the Negev, Be'er Sheva	1969	5,500
Weizmann Institute of Science, Rehovot	1934	5,000

Fig. 10. Universities of Israel.

The Open University
Established in 1974 and patterned on the British model, the Open University offers distinctive, non-traditional higher education opportunities towards a bachelor degree by utilizing flexible methods based primarily on self-study textbooks and guides, supplemented by structured assignments and periodic tutorials, with final examinations.

Colleges and seminaries
Regional colleges, situated mainly in non-urban areas, offer academic courses under the auspices of one of the universities, making it possible for students to begin studying for a degree near their home and complete it at the university's main campus. A number of colleges, six of which specialise in music, fashion, business administration, technology and the administration of co-operatives, grant bachelor degrees. Six teacher training seminaries award bachelor of education degrees in general education, as well as in the teaching of sports, music, technology, science and so on.

Useful telephone numbers
Technion-Israel Institute of Technology, Haifa. Tel: 04 8292111/ 3111.

	Bar Ilan University	Ben Gurion University	Hebrew University	Technion-Israel Institute of Technology	Tel Aviv University	University of Haifa	Weizmann Institute of Science	The Open University
Humanities	✓	✓	✓		✓	✓		✓
Social Sciences	✓	✓	✓	✓	✓	✓		✓
Business Administration	✓	✓	✓		✓	✓		
Economics	✓	✓	✓	✓	✓	✓		
Psychology	✓	✓	✓		✓	✓		✓
Library Science	✓		✓					
Law	✓		✓		✓	✓		
Arts	✓		✓		✓	✓		
Social Work	✓	✓	✓		✓	✓		
Education	✓	✓	✓	✓	✓	✓		
Mathematics and Computers	✓	✓	✓	✓	✓	✓	✓	✓
Natural Sciences	✓	✓	✓	✓	✓	✓	✓	✓
Engineering		✓		✓	✓			
Architecture				✓				
Agriculture			✓	✓				
Medicine		✓	✓	✓	✓			
Dentistry			✓	✓	✓			
Veterinary Medicine			✓					
Pharmacy and Pharmacology		✓	✓					
Physiotherapy		✓			✓			
Nursing		✓	✓		✓			

Fig. 11. Fields of study in the universities.

Haifa University, Haifa. Tel: 04 8240111.
Hebrew University, Jerusalem. Tel: 02 6585111.
Bar-Ilan University, Ramat Gan, Tel: 03 5318111.
Tel Aviv University, Ramat Aviv. Tel: 03 6408111.
Ben Gurion University of the Negev, Be'er Sheva Tel: 07 6461111.
Weizmann Institute of Science, Rehovot. Tel: 08 9342111.
The Open University, Tel Aviv. Tel: 03 6460460.

University Trusts in Britain
Friends of the Hebrew University of Jerusalem, 3 St John's Wood
    Road, London NW8 8RB. Tel: (0171) 286 1176. Fax: (0171) 289
    5549.
Tel Aviv University Trust, 1 Bentinck Street, London W1M 5RN.
    Tel: (0171) 487 5280. Fax: (0171) 224 3908.
British Friends of Haifa University, 26 Enford Street, London W1H
    2DD. Tel: (0171) 724 3777.
Ben Gurion University Foundation, 22 Grosvenor Street, London
    W1X 9FE. Tel: (0171) 499 2276. Fax: (0171) 491 2649.
British Technion Society, 62 Grosvenor Street, London W1X 9DA.
    Tel: (0171) 495 6824. Fax: (0171) 355 1525.
Weizmann Institute Foundation, 14–15 Rodmarton Street, London
    W1 3FW. Tel: (0171) 486 3954. Fax: (0171) 268 2629.
Friends of Bar Illan University, 16 Wigmore Street, London W1H
    9DE. Tel: (0171) 436 9706. Fax: (0171) 436 483.

Choosing the right university
When coming to choose a university, the first thing you need is
information. Each university publishes a handbook and guide for
students; get one from the register office. A very useful publication is
Higher Education in Israel: a Guide for Overseas Students which is
published by the Department of Information for Olim. Another
useful publication is *Courses in Israel* (trilingual) which is published
by the Department of International Cooperation, and which
contains information about different courses. Figure 11 summarises
the variety of fields of study offered by the different universities.

Useful addresses
Ministry of Education and Culture, Jerusalem 9191.
Ministry of Foreign Affairs, Cultural and Scientific Relations
    Division, Jerusalem 91950.
Ministry of Immigrant Absorption, Students' Authority, 6 Hillel
    Street, Jerusalem 94581.

Israeli Student Tourist Association (ISTA), 109 Ben Yehuda Street, Tel Aviv. 31 Ha'neviim Street, Jerusalem.
Office of Overseas Students Admissions, Hebrew University of Jerusalem, Mount Scopus, Jerusalem 91905.
The Department of Information for Olim, PO Box 616, Jerusalem.
The Department of International Cooperation, Ministry of Foreign Affairs, Jerusalem 91950.

Taking location and accommodation into account
Another very important consideration in choosing a university is its location. If you wish, for example, to live in Jerusalem it would be foolish to enrol in Haifa. You need to remember that you will not necessarily be admitted to the university of your choice. Admission to specific courses can sometimes be very difficult (the law for example) and your chance of getting a place depends on your high school marks and the results of a psychological test which is done before the start of the academic year. (You can take this examination in Britain; contact the Israeli consulate.) It is important, therefore, that you apply to as many universities as possible.
The possibility of obtaining student accommodation is another important factor to consider. Student accommodation is usually cheaper, close to the university (thus saving money on transportation) and socially very convenient, especially for foreigners.

Scholarships
Higher education in Israel is quite expensive and it is helpful if you can supplement your budget with a scholarship. Here is a list of some that are available:

1. *Ministry of Foreign Affairs*
Governmental scholarships (60)
Address: Jerusalem 91950.
Subjects: All major subjects.
Tenable: All Israeli institutions of higher education.
Eligible: Applicants holding a BA; maximum age 35, proficiency English and Hebrew.
Duration: One academic year.
Value: US $500 per month plus medical insurance.
Applications: By 15 November; send to the Israeli embassy.

2. *Institute of Jewish Studies, Hebrew University, Jerusalem*
Moritz and Charlotte Warburg prize (15).

Address: (The Secretary) Mount Scopus, Jerusalem 91905.
Subjects: Jewish studies; graduate and postgraduate.
Open to: Nationals of all countries.
Duration: One year (renewable).
Value: US $6,500 to $7,000 per year.
Applications: By the end of November to the above address.

3. *Lady Davis Fellowship (a) Graduate and Postdoctoral Fellowships
    (b) Visiting Professorships*
    Address: (The Secretary) PO Box 1255, Jerusalem 91904.
    Subjects: All fields of study – Hebrew University and Technion,
    Haifa.
    Tenable: (a) At the Hebrew University Jerusalem. (b) At the
    Technion, Haifa.
    Open to: Only students who are enrolled in a PhD programme
    overseas are eligible applicants for the fellowship at the Hebrew
    University; applicants for the Technion must have completed
    their studies with excellent marks.
    Duration: (a) One academic year; extension for a second year
    requires approval of the Academic committee.(b) From one
    semester to a full academic year.
    Value: (a) Graduate award covers cost of travel and tuition as well as
    reasonable living expenses; postdoctoral award covers cost of
    travel for Fellow, plus a monthly stipend equivalent to a
    lecturer's salary at the Hebrew University and Technion. (b)
    Grant includes a professorial salary plus travel costs.
    Applications: By 1 December.

CASE STUDIES

Clair is now in her second year at the Hebrew University
Her Hebrew is pretty good now and she, at last, understands the
lectures. She is still allowed to submit written works in English, but
she hopes to be able to submit in Hebrew in the next year. Clair
plans to go back to England when she completed her studies in the
summer of next year.

John is now travelling with his second-hand car
He is now in the Sinai after spending a month in Jordan. When he is
back in Isreal he will travel a bit more, and then sell his car and go
back to England.

Jill is planning to return to England at Christmas
In two weeks time she will stop working and leave her flat. She will then travel in Israel and return home.

DISCUSSION POINTS

1. Draw up a list of questions you intend to ask the headteacher at the nursery you want to visit.

2. Look at the list of choices in high school and decide which track you want your son/daughter to follow.

3. Look at the list of choices in higher education and see which institution suits you best. Then send a letter asking for more information.

10
Doing Business in Israel

WHY DO BUSINESS IN ISRAEL?

Israel's economy is now growing very fast at a rate of 6 per cent annually. Inflation is relatively low and so is unemployment. A fast growing market is where opportunities are to be found and Israel offers opportunities for businessmen/women and investors alike.

British-Israeli business relations
British-Israeli business relations have improved dramatically in the last three years or so. Israel is Britain's second largest trading partner in the Middle East; Britain is Israel's second largest trading partner after the United States.

Some big British companies have already started to invest in Israel. **British Telecom** and **Cable & Wireless** are both bidding for roles in Israel's telecommunications market and the Edinburgh-based **Martin Currie Investment Management** has recently increased its holding in Israel. The Anglo-Dutch foods-to-soap conglomerate **Unilever** has recently acquired a 50 per cent stake in Strauss Dairies, Israel's leading ice cream manufacturer which has annual sales of about $60 million. The British **Ministry of Defence** has concluded a multi-million deal to buy Israeli-made ammunition. **Carlton Communications** plc announced the $52 million case sale of Avekas Video systems to Israel's Scitex corporation which produces state-of-the-art electronic publishing technology.

CONDUCTING BUSINESS IN ISRAEL

Understanding different practices and customs
Israel does offer opportunities but investing and doing business can be a challenging and frustrating task. The main problem for you, the foreign investor or business[wo]man, is likely to be the Israeli style which presents a more personal approach of making business than

rigid professionalism.

You might find it frustrating, for example, when you are unable to get a positive reply to a straightforward question. In addition, the *Pakid*, the clerk who represents the Israeli bureaucracy, tends not to make matters easier for the foreigner.

Generally speaking, it is usual to make appointments for business contacts, and to use business cards. Israelis, however, tend not to be punctual and you may find yourself kept waiting for as long as half an hour or even more. You will also find that Israelis are eager to cut corners. It may take some time until an Israeli businessman decides to move ahead, but when he does he will usually like to see things moving very fast.

Informality
Informality is perhaps the most outstanding characteristic of the Israeli way of doing business. Informality is manifested, for example, in the way an Israeli businessman is dressed; he can come to an important meeting with open-necked and short-sleeved shirt. You will find that there is much less emphasis on status, ranking and titles and those at the top are relatively accessible.

Doing it the Israeli way
Deals are rarely agreed over the phone. A typical Israeli business-man would want to see you and meet with you face to face. When coming to a meeting with an Israeli businessman, do not expect to find him or her in a spectacular office. This is not part of the Israeli style and you may well find Israeli offices rather shabby and business lunches short (lacking wine and other spirits!). Things are changing and managers of big businesses do have somewhat stylish offices, but still much less than in Britain.

Smoothing the process
Doing business in Israel is first and foremost knowing the right people and having personal contacts with those who can help you avoid the pitfalls which could derail your efforts. Always try to locate the key persons in the organisation and try meeting them face to face. It is all right to ask for their help in sorting out all kinds of problems. Straightforwardness and openness can solve many difficulties.

Ha'maté le-kidum asakim
To help foreign business[wo]men and potential advisers, the Trade and Industry Ministry established the *Maté le-kidum asakim* which

aims to locate foreign investors and help them cope with all the difficulties in establishing their business and investment in Israel. *For details contact*: Ha'maté le-kidum asakim, 8 King David Road, Jerusalem. Tel: 02 5861707.

Conferences

Israel's record as an international conference centre began in 1963, and the country now attracts about 150 international meetings a year with 50,000 delegates. Scientific and academic meetings account for about half the meetings, though religious and sporting events are on the increase.

In Tel Aviv there are seven hotels with substantial convention and meetings facilities, along with the Israel Trade Fairs and Convention Centre and the Kfar Maccabiah Hotel Convention and Sports Centre which offers 19 banqueting rooms accommodating up to 1,000 people. In Haifa, the Haifa Exhibition and Convention Centre is set to open in 1996 with 8,000 sq m of exhibition hall space and a main convention hall that will be able to accommodate up to 2,500 participants.

Apart from hotels and convention centres in Tel Aviv and Jerusalem, opportunities exist to hold meetings in Kibbutzim.

For more information contact: The International Conventions Department, Ministry of Tourism, 24 King George Street, Jerusalem 91009. Tel: 02 6754811.

INVESTING IN ISRAEL

Banks

A good bank can not only advise you how to invest your money but also act as your go-between and direct you in the maze of Israeli business and investment.

When the state of Israel was established in 1948 there were 150 banks in the country, most of which belonged to families or institutions. But in the late 1960s the big banks, encouraged by the Central Bank of Israel, swallowed most of the small ones. Nowadays there are four big banks and only six private banks in Israel. The advantage of the small banks is that if they see you as a good client they will go out of their way to help you, and while in the big bank you will be served by a clerk, in the small bank you might have direct access to the manager himself.

The four big banks

Bank Ha'poalim
Head Office and Central Branch, 50 Rothschild Boulevard, Tel Aviv.
Tel: 03 5673333.
Tourist Department, 104 Ha'yarkon Street, Tel Aviv. Tel: 03 5200606.

Bank Leumi
Tel Aviv central branch, 19 Herzel Street. Tel: 03 5148111. Fax: 5661872.
Jerusalem, 19 Ha'melech David Street. Tel: 02 6201811.

Israel Discount Bank Ltd
Head Office, 27 Yehuda Ha'levi Street, Tel Aviv. Tel: 03 5145555.
Tourist Centre and main foreign exchange branch, 71 Ben Yehuda Street, Tel Aviv. Tel: 03 5203177.

The First International Bank
Head Office, 9 Ahad Ha'am Street, Tel Aviv. Tel: 03 5196111. Fax: 03 5100316.

Six small banks

Israel General Bank Ltd
Tel Aviv, 38 Rothschild Boulevard. Tel: 03 5645645.
Haifa, 5 Khait Street. Tel: 04 8625111.
Jerusalem, 32 Keren Ha'yesod Street. Tel: 02 5600200.
Director General: Eli Yunis. 53 per cent of the shares of this bank, the largest of the small employing 185 people, are owned by the French Rothschild family. The bank, which has three branches, works with big businessmen.

Euro Trade Bank
41 Rothschild Boulevard, PO Box 37318, Tel Aviv. Tel: 03 5643838.
Fax: 03 5602483.
Manager: Menachem Weber. This private bank which employs 28 people and has one branch in Tel Aviv, offers all banking services apart from cash. It has about 150 clients.

The Maritime Bank of Israel Ltd
Tel Aviv, 35 Ahad Ha'am Street Tel: 03 5642222. Fax: 03 5642323.

Manager: Amir Geva. This private bank, which employs 70 people, was owned in the past by the government to finance maritime business in Israel. The bank has about 2,000 clients.

Bank Le'mischar Ltd
Tel Aviv, 42 Lilenblum Street. Tel: 5647888.
Manager: Eliahu Hunger. The bank was established in 1936 and is now controlled by Shmil Weber, an Austrian Jew, who holds 50 per cent of the shares. The bank has 55 employees and 2,000 clients. In addition to its Tel Aviv branch it has one in Be'er Sheva.

Bank Polska Kasa Opieki Tel Aviv (Bank Pekao) Ltd
Tel Aviv, 95 Allenby Street. Tel: 03 5663641. Fax: 03 5660840; 5660916; 5663641.
This Polish bank was established in 1933 to support the needs of Polish Jews who immigrated to Palestine. The bank has one branch, 40 employees and 2,000 clients.

Bank O'lami Le'haskahot
Petha Tikva, 48 Ho'vevai Zion. Tel: 03 9311222; 9308116.
Director General: Moshe Mendalbaum. The bank has 1,000 clients and is headed by the former General Comptroller of The Bank of Israel.

TRANSFERRING MONEY

If you need to transfer money from or to Israel you can do it either through your bank or by using the post.

The postal authority **Western Union**'s agent in Israel is one of the ways to transfer money. Western Union works both ways. To send money to Israel, the sender enters any Western Union branch abroad, fills out a form and pays the required cash and service charge. If you are the receiver, you may, with proof of identity, collect the money in cash in NIS from any designated postal branch in Israel. You do not need a bank account.

If you wish to send money abroad, you need to fill out a form at any designated postal branch and pay the required cash and service charge. The transaction will be processed to a branch of Western Union abroad. You can find the telephone number in any directory under 'Western Union Money Transfer'. In Israel the toll-free number is 177 022 2131.

WORKING HOURS AND HOLIDAYS

Israel's business hours vary in line with the Shabath and Jewish festivals. On the Shabath shops, offices and banks are closed; some reopen on Saturday evening. Services like buses and railways close down on Friday afternoon and Saturday (the exception is Haifa where buses are running even on the Shabath). For Jews the day begins in the evening, so that a Jewish festival begins at sunset on the previous day and ends at sunset on the day of the festival. Working hours are usually from 0800 to 1800; Friday from 0800 to 1400.

Public holidays

The system of public holidays in Israel is quite complicated since there are Jewish, Christian and Muslim holidays. Jewish and Muslim festivals are regulated by lunar calendars so that from year to year they occur at different dates in the Gregorian calendar (see Figure 12).

Festival	1996	1997	1998	1999	2000
Too Bi'shvat	5.2	23.1	11.2	1.2	22.1
Purim	5.3	23.3	12.3	2.3	21.3
1 Pesach	4.4	22.4	11.4	1.4	20.4
8 Pesach	10.4	28.4	17.4	7.4	26.4
Independence	24.4	12.5	30.4	21.4	10.5
Lag Ba'omer	7.5	25.5	14.5	4.5	23.5
Shavuot	24.5	11.6	31.5	21.5	9.6
Rosh Ha'shana	14–15.9	2–3.10	21–22.9	11–12.9	30.9–1.10
Yom Kippur	23.9	11.10	30.9	20.9	9.10
Sukot	29.9	16.10	5.10	25.9	14.10
Simhat Tora	5.10	23.10	12.10	2.10	2.10
Hanuka	6.12	24.12	14.12	4.12	22.12

Fig. 12. Israel's festivals 1996–2000.

COMMUNICATIONS

Making a telephone call

The old-fashioned Israeli telephones in which you used tokens called *assimons* are disappearing. Most telephones now take magnetic phone cards which you can buy in post offices and kiosks. They are in units of 10, 20, 50, 120 or 240. Charges vary according to the time of day; highest rates are from 0830 to 1300; medium rates from 1300 to 2100; cheap rates from 2100 to 0800, on Friday from 1300 and on Saturday. When calling in Israel and out of the area where you are situated you need to use an area code. Here are some of these codes:

City	Area code
Afula	06
Ashdod	08
Eilat	07
Haifa	04
Hezliyya	09
Jerusalem	02
Netanya	09
Tel Aviv	03
Tiberias	06

You can find more area codes in the *Yellow Pages* or in any telephone directory.

Some words and phrases for a telephone conversation

English	Hebrew
Hello	Sha-lom
My name is...	Sh-mi...
I am from Britain	A-ni me-Bri-ta-nya
I am living in...	An-ni Gar-B...
Good morning	Bo-ker Tov
Good evening	E-rev Tov
Good night	La-yla Tov
Today	Ha-yom
Tomorrow	Ma-char
Yesterday	Et-mol
Do you speak English?	Ha-im Ata Me-da-ber An-glit?
Sorry, but I do not understand	S-licha a-val ani lo me-vin
Can we meet?	Ha-im ef-shar le-i-pa-gesh?

Where?	Ei-fo?
When?	Ma-tai?
What?	Maa?
At what time?	Be-eizé Sha-aa?
I am looking for a job	A-ni me-cha-pes A-vo-da
See you later	Le-i-tra-ot
Yes	Ken
No	Lo
Please	Be-va-ka-sha
Thank you	To-da

Making international calls

It is possible to make international calls from public telephones by using **Telecard**; some telephones also accept credit cards. You will pay 50 per cent less in calls to many European countries, including Britain, if you call between 0100 and 0800. You will have a reduction of 25 per cent if you call between Monday and Friday between 2200 and 0100 and on Saturday and Sunday from 0800 until 0100 (17 hours). If you dial to the United States (including Alaska and Hawaii) and Canada during the week you will have 45 per cent reduction on calls which are made between 2400 and 0800. You will have 20 per cent reduction if you ring between Monday and Friday from 0800 and 1300 and on Saturday and Sunday from 0800 and 2400 (16 hours).

- Do remember the time difference between Israel and Britain. You can find out about it in the *Yellow Pages* and in telephone directories.

- To ring from the UK to Israel dial: 00-972-area code without 0 - your number.

- From Israel to the UK dial: 00-44-area code without 0 - your number.

Telephone services

Wake-up service	174, 175
Information on phone numbers	144
Speaking clock (what's the time)	155
Information on aircraft landings	03 9723333 (Hebrew);
	03 9723344 (English)
Weather forecast	03 9668855
Overseas operator	188

Telephone out of order   166
Telegrams   171

Post offices

You can identify a post office by the leaping figure of a white stag on a blue background. Head post offices are open Sunday–Tuesday and Thursday between 0800 and 1800, branch offices from 0800 to 1230 and from 1530 to 1800; Wednesday from 0800 to 1330 and Friday from 0800 to 1300 or 1400.

You can buy stamps in each post office (as well as stationery and souvenir shops and bookshops). Mail can be sent *Post Restante* to any head post office. In Jerusalem at 23 Jaffa Road; in Tel Aviv, 132 Allenby Street.

Post boxes are either yellow for local mail or red for all other destinations. Delivery time for mail in Israel is between one and two days; international approximately one week, unless you send it via a quicker method. For more information ask in any post office.

You can also use head post offices to send telegrams round the clock; you can also do it by telephoning 171.

DISCUSSION POINTS

1. Put in your diary the dates of Jewish and Moslem festivals which might affect your business in Israel.

2. Compare between the big and small banks and see which one might best suit your business.

Glossary

Aliya. Literally 'ascent'. Jewish/Israeli immigration to Palestine/Israel.

Ashkenazim. Jews and their descendants originating from Central and Eastern Europe.

Beit Knesset. Synagogue.

Diaspora. The Jewish community living worldwide.

Eretz Yisrael. 'The land of Israel.' The traditional Jewish term for Palestine.

Green Line. The pre-1967 border between Israel and its neighbours.

Ha'gana. 'Defence.' The Jewish underground organisation in Palestine during the British Mandate.

'Ha'shetachim'. The territories occupied by Israel in 1967.

Hassid. "Righteous or pious", someone belonging to an ultra orthodox Jewish sect.

Histadrut. Israel Federation of Labour, encompassing trade union, major co-operative and economic enterprises and a sick fund.

IDF. Israeli Defence Forces, the armed forces of Israel, established 1948.

Intifada. The Palestinian uprising on the West Bank and Gaza.

Kfar. Small village.

Kibbutz. Collective settlement.

Kipa. Skullcap.

Knesset. The Israeli Parliament.

Kosher. Food prepared according to the Jewish dietary laws.

Likud. The word means 'being together'. A right-wing political party.

Ma'arach. A left of the centre political party.

Menorah. Seven-pronged candelabra; an ancient Jewish symbol associated with the Hanuka Festival.

Mishnah. The legal codification of basic Jewish law – the Ha'lacha.

Mitnadev. Volunteer.

Moshav. Co-operative smallholders's settlement combining features of both co-operative and private agriculture.

Ole Hadash. A new immigrant.

Sabra. A prickly cactus which is sweet inside. The word is used as a nickname for native Israelis.

Sherut. Shared taxi.

Shuq. Market.

Torah. Moses's five books.

Ulpan. School for Hebrew.

Yad. Hand, also used for memorial.

Yarmulka. Skullcap.

Yeshiva. Jewish religious seminary.

Yom Kippur. The Day of Atonement. The most sacred day for Jews.

Further Reading

ABOUT ISRAEL AND THE ISRAELIS

Aharoni, Yair, *The Israeli Economy: Dreams and Realities* (London, 1991).
Arian, Asher, *Politics in Israel – The Second Generation* (New Jersey, 1995).
Bellow, Saul, *To Jerusalem and Back* (New York, 1976).
Ben Sasson, Haim, *A History of the Jewish People* (Cambridge, 1976).
Eban, Abba, *My Country: The Story of Modern Israel* (London, 1972).
Elon, Amos, *The Israelis: Founders and Sons* (London, 1971).
Grossman, David, *Sleeping on a Wire: Conversations with Palestinians in Israel* (London, 1990).
Herzog, Haim, *The Arab-Israel Wars: War and Peace in the Middle East – From the War of Independence Through Lebanon* (New York, 1984).
Mikes, George, *The Prophet Motive: Israel Today and Tomorrow* (London, 1969).
Oz, Amos, *In the Land of Israel* (London, 1983).
Oz, Amos, *The Slopes of Lebanon* (London, 1990).
Rolef, S. Hattis, *Political Dictionary of the State of Israel* (New York, 1987)
Sachar, Howard, *A History of Israel: From the Rise of Zionism to our Time* (New York, 1976).
Said, Edward, *The Question of Palestine* (London, 1979).

FOR EXPATS

Jones, Roger, *Obtaining Visas & Work Permits* (How To Books, 1996).
Jones, Roger, *How to Emigrate* (How To Books, 1994).
Briggs, Rod, *Working on Contract Worldwide* (How To Books, 1996).
Golding, Jonathan, *Working Abroad: Essential Financial Planning for Expatriates and their Employers* (How To Books, 1994).

Useful Addresses

COMMERCIAL ORGANISATIONS

Bank of Israel, Eliezer Street, Kiryat Ben Gurion, Jerusalem. Tel: 02 6552211.

Israel–British Chamber of Commerce, 76 Iben Gvirol, Tel Aviv, 64162. Tel: 03 6959732.

Histadrut–General Federation of Labour in Israel, 93 Arloseroff Street, Tel Aviv, 62098. Tel: 03 6921111, 6921630.

Manufacturers' Association of Israel, Tel Aviv, PO Box 29116. Tel: 03 5198787.

Israel and British Commonwealth Assocation, 76, Iben Gvirol Street, Tel Aviv, PO Box 4090. Tel: 03 6265244.

Federation of Israeli Chambers of Commerce, 84 Ha'hashmonaim Street, Tel Aviv, 67011. Tel: 03 5612444.

POLITICAL PARTIES

Israel Labour Party, 110 Ha'yarkon Street, Tel Aviv. Tel: 03 5209222.

The Likud, Metsudat Ze'ev, 38 King George Street, Tel Aviv. Tel: 03 6210666.

National Religious Party, 4 Markin Street, Ramat Gan. Tel: 03 6702541.

Agudat Yisrael, 5 Harav Orenstein Yitzhak, Jerusalem. Tel: 02 5384357.

Se'pharadi Torah Guardians (Shas), 20 Aliav Street, Jerusalem. Tel: 02 5371786.

Ha'dash, 17 Tirtza Street, Tel Aviv. Tel: 03 6835252.

Shinui, 22 Mikve Yisrael Street, Tel Aviv. Tel: 03 614737.

Tzomet, 44 Derech Petach Tikva, Tel Aviv. Tel: 03 6393786.

Mo'ledet, 23 Ha'melech George, Jerusalem. Tel: 02 6249195.

The Third Way, 8 Kaplan Street, Tel Aviv. Tel: 03 6950052.

Yisrael Be'aliya, 40 Derech Petach Tikva, Tel Aviv. Tel: 03 6874998.

OFFICES OF THE MINISTRY OF INTERIOR (FOR EXTENSION OF VISA)

Jerusalem, 1 Shlomzion Ha'malka Street. Tel: 02 90222.

Tel Aviv, Shalom Tower, 9 Ahad Ha'am Street. Tel: 03 5193333.

Haifa, 11 Hasson Shuqri Street. Tel: 04 8616222.

TRAVELLING TO ISRAEL – AIR

The Air Travel Advisory Bureau (for free advice on air travel). Tel: (0171) 636 5000 (London) or (0161) 832 2000 (Manchester).

West End Travel Ltd, Barratt House, 341 Oxford Street, London W1R 1HB. Tel: (0171) 629 6299 (main switchboard); (0171) 409 0630 (Israel Department).

El Al. Tel: (0171) 437 8237 (London).

British Airways. Tel: (0181) 759 5511 (London).

STA, the students' travel agency. Tel: 02 6222333 (Jerusalem); (0171) 361 6161 (London).

Ben Gurion International Airport. Tel: 03 9710000 (for general information); 03 9723333 or 03 9710111 (record – arrival and departures).

Ovda Airport (south). Tel: 07 6375880.

Eilat Airport (south). Tel: 07 6371828.

Israel Airports Authority, PO Box 137, Ben Gurion International Airport, 70100, Lod. Tel: 03 9710000.

TRAVELLING TO ISRAEL – LAND

Border Crossing Egypt	The Rafiah Terminal. Tel: 07 6734205.
	The Taba Terminal. Tel: 07 6373100; 07 6372104.
Border Crossing Jordan	Allenby Bridge. Tel: 02 9942302.
	Arava Crossing. Tel: 07 6336811.

TRAVELLING TO ISRAEL – COMING WITH YOUR YACHT

Yacht marinas
Atarim (Tel Aviv). Tel: 03 5254276.
Yaffo (Jaffa). Tel: 03 6820772.
Akko (Acre). Tel: 04 9919287.
Eilat. Tel: 07 6367186.

CUSTOMS

The Department of Customs, 32 Agron Street, 91002, Jerusalem. Tel: 02 6703333.

GETTING AROUND IN ISRAEL – INTERNAL FLIGHTS

1. Arkia
Eilat, 1001 Ha'kanyon Ha'adom. Tel: 07 6373388.
Haifa, 84 Ha'atzmaut Street. Tel: 04 8643371.

Jerusalem, Clal Centre, 97 Jaffa Road. Tel: 02 6255888.
Netanya, 10 Stemper Street. Tel: 09 843143.
Rosh Pinna Airport. Tel: 06 936478.
Tel Aviv, Sde Dov Airport. Tel: 03 9602222/3333.

2. Snunit Aviation
Tel: 03 699 3184.

TRAVELLING AROUND IN ISRAEL – BUS (TO FIND OUT ABOUT SCHEDULES, TICKETS AND PRICES)

Tel Aviv. Tel: 03 5375555.
Jerusalem. Tel: 02 5304555.
Haifa. Tel: 04 8549555.

TRAVELLING AROUND IN ISRAEL – TRAIN (TO FIND OUT ABOUT SCHEDULES, TICKETS AND PRICES)

Tel Aviv. Tel: 03 5622200.
Haifa. Tel: 04 8303133.

TRAVELLING AROUND IN ISRAEL – CAR RENTAL

Ben Gurion Airport: Budget. Tel: 03 9711504/5. Hertz. Tel: 03 9711165/6.
Eldan. Tel: 03 9721027/8. Europcar. Tel: 03 9721097.
Tel Aviv: Avis, 12 Ha'masger Street. Tel: 03 6360000. Budget, 99 Ha'yarkon
Street. Tel: 03 5227741. Eldan, 40 Ha'masger Street. Tel: 03 6394343.
And 112 Ha'yarkon Street. Tel: 03 5271166. Europcar, 126 Ha'yarkon
Street. Tel: 03 5248181. Hertz, 10 Karlibach Street. Tel: 03 6841010.
Jerusalem: Budget, 24 King David Street. Tel: 02 6248902. Eldan, 24 King
David Street. Tel: 02 6257555. Europcar, 18 King David Street. Tel: 02
6256334.

STUDYING HEBREW IN ISRAEL

Division of Adult Education, Beit Ha'am, 11 Betzalel Street, Jerusalem,
94591. Tel: 02 6254157.
YMHA (Hebrew Youth Centre), 105 Herzog Street, Jerusalem. Tel: 02
789441 or 02 780442.
Mo'adon Ha'ole, 9 Alkalay Street, Jerusalem. Tel: 02 5633718.
Beit Mitchell, 17 Straus Street, Jerusalem. Tel: 02 6257950.
Ulpan Akiva, PO Box 6086, 42160 Netanya. Tel: 09 352312.

PUTTING YOUR ADS IN A NEWSPAPER

Dahaf. Tel: 02 6256355.
The Jerusalem Post. Tel: 02 5315666.
Yediot Ahronot. Tel: 03 6972222.
Ha'aretz. Tel: 03 9648750.
Maariv. Tel: 03 5632111.

WORKING IN THE KIBBUTZ AND MOSHAV

Kibbutz Representatives (London Office), 1A Accommodation Road, London NW11 8ED. Tel: (0181) 458 9235.
Kibbutz Representatives (Tel Aviv Office), 18 Frischman Street. Tel: 03 5278874.
Manchester interview address, Peltours Ltd, 27–29 Church Street, Manchester M4 1QA.
Glasgow interview address, 222 Fenwick Road, Giffnock, Glasgow G46 6UE.
Project 67 (London office), 10 Hatton Garden, London EC1N 8AH. Tel: (0171) 831 7626. Fax: (0171) 404 5588.
Project 67 (Tel Aviv office), 94 Ben Yehuda Street, Tel Aviv. Tel: 03 5230140.
The Takam (United Kibbutz Movement) Volunteers Department, 18 Frischman Street, Tel Aviv. Tel: 03 5246154.
Ha'kibbutz Ha'dati (The Religious Kibbutzim Movement), 7 Dobnov Street, Tel Aviv. Tel: 03 6957231.

WORKING IN ISRAEL

Star Au Pair International, 16 Michal Street, Tel Aviv 63261. Tel: 03 6291748, 03 6201195, 052 452002 (David Star).
Au Pair International, 2 Desler Street, B'nei B'rak 51507. Tel: 03 6190423.
'Babayit' nannies and foreign workers, 26 Rambam Street, Tel Aviv. Tel: 03 5289990. 62/5 Bialik Street, Ramat Gan. Tel: 03 6720697. 17 Hovevai Zion Street, Petach Tikva. Tel: 03 9340275.
Danel, 98 Dizingoff Street, Tel Aviv. Tel: 03 5222266.

EMERGENCY NUMBERS

First Aid, Emergency. Tel: 101.
Intensive care ambulance service. Tel: 03 5460111 (Tel Aviv). 02 561303 (Jerusalem). 04 8672222 (Haifa).
Shaal. Tel: 03 5625555.

Other medical services
Eran, Mental Health Hotline. Tel: 1201.
Rape Crisis Centre. Tel: 04 8530533.
Open Door, sex advice for youth. Tel: 03 5101411.
Hand in Hand, Child Hotline. Tel: 03 5226027.
Alcoholics Anonymous. Tel: 03 5225255.
Narcotics Anonymous. Tel: 03 5758869.

DISABLED

The Royal Association for Disability and Rehabilitation (RADAR), 25
    Mortimer Street, London W1N 8AB. Tel: (0171) 637 5400.
The Spinal Injuries Association, 76 St James's Lane, London N10 3DF. Tel:
    (0181) 444 2122.
Mobility International, 62 Union Street, London SE1. Tel: (0171) 403 5688.
Milbat, The Advisory Centre for the Disabled, Sheeba Medical Centre, Tel
    Aviv. Tel: 03 5303739.
Yad Sarah, 43 Ha'neviim Street, 95141 Jerusalem. Tel: 02 244242. Fax: 02
    244493.

EDUCATION

Technion-Israel Institute of Technology, Haifa. Tel: 04 8292111/3111.
Haifa University, Haifa. Tel: 04 8240111.
Hebrew University, Jerusalem. Tel: 02 6585111.
Bar-Ilan University, Ramat Gan. Tel: 03 5318111.
Tel Aviv University, Ramat Aviv. Tel: 03 6408111.
Ben Gurion University of the Negev, Be'er Sheva. Tel: 07 6461111.
Weizmann Institute of Science, Rehovot. Tel: 08 9342111.
The Open University, Tel Aviv. Tel: 03 6460460.

University Trusts in Britain
Friends of the Hebrew University of Jerusalem, 3 St John's Wood Road,
    London NW8 8RB. Tel: (0171) 286 1176. Fax: (0171) 289 5549.
Tel Aviv University Trust, 1 Bentinck Street, London W1M 5RN. Tel:
    (0171) 487 5280. Fax: (0171) 224 3908.
British Friends of Haifa University, 26 Enford Street, London W1H 2DD.
    Tel: (0171) 724 3777.
Ben Gurion University Foundation, 22 Grosvenor Street, London W1X
    9FE. Tel: (0171) 499 2276. Fax: (0171) 491 2649.
British Technion Society, 62 Grosvenor Street, London W1X 9DA. Tel:
    (0171) 495 6824. Fax: (0171) 355 1525.
Weizmann Institute Foundation, 14–15 Rodmarton Street, London W1
    3FW. Tel: (0171) 486 3954. Fax: (0171) 268 2629.

Friends of the Bar-Ilan University, 16 Wigmore Street, London W1H 9DE. Tel: (0171) 436 9706. Fax: (0171) 436 483.

BUSINESS

The International Conventions Department, Ministry of Tourism, 24 King George Street, Jerusalem 91009. Tel: 02 6754811.
Ha'maté le-kidum asakim, 8 King David Road, Jerusalem. Tel: 02 5861707.

Banks

Bank Ha'poalim, Head Office and Central Branch, 50 Rothschild Boulevard, Tel Aviv. Tel: 03 5673333. Tourist Department, 104 Ha'yarkon Street, Tel Aviv. Tel: 03 5200606.
Bank Leumi, Tel Aviv central branch, 19 Herzel Street. Tel: 03 5148111. Fax: 03 5661872. Jerusalem, 19 Ha'melech David Street. Tel: 02 6201811.
Israel Discount Bank Ltd, Head Office, 27 Yehuda Ha'levi Street, Tel Aviv. Tel: 03 5145555. Tourist centre and main foreign exchange branch, 71 Ben Yehuda Street, Tel Aviv. Tel: 03 5203177.
The First International Bank, Head Office, 9 Ahad Ha'am Street, Tel Aviv. Tel: 03 5196111. Fax: 03 5100316.
Israel General Bank Ltd, Tel Aviv, 38 Rothschild Boulevard. Tel: 03 5645645. Haifa, 5 Khiat Street. Tel: 04 8625111. Jerusalem, 32 Keren Ha'yesod Street. Tel: 02 5600200.
Euro Trade Bnank, 41 Rothschild Boulevard, PO Box 37318. Tel: 03 5643838. Fax: 03 5602483.
The Maritime Bank of Israel Ltd, Tel Aviv, 35 Ahad Ha'am Street. Tel: 03 5642222. Fax: 03 5642323.
Bank Le'mischar Ltd, Tel Aviv, 42 Lilenblum Street. Tel: 03 5647888.
Bank Polska Kasa Opieki Tel Aviv (Bank Pekao) Ltd, Tel Aviv, 95 Allenby Street. Tel. 03 5663641.
Bank O'lami Le'haskahot, Petha Tikva, 48 Ho'vevai Zion. Tel: 03 9311222, 9308116.

Index